THE FLATLANDERS

AMERICAN MUSIC SERIES

Peter Blackstock and David Menconi, *Editors*

The FLATLANDERS

Now It's Now Again

JOHN T. DAVIS

UNIVERSITY OF TEXAS PRESS ❧ AUSTIN

Requests for permission to reproduce material
from this work should be sent to:
> Permissions
> University of Texas Press
> P.O. Box 7819
> Austin, TX 78713-7819
> http://utpress.utexas.edu/index.php/rp-form

The paper used in this book meets the minimum requirements
of ANSI/NISO Z39.48-1992 (R1997) (Permanence of Paper). ∞

Design by Lindsay Starr

LIBRARY OF CONGRESS CATALOGING-IN-PUBLICATION DATA

Davis, John T. (John Terry), 1955–   author.
  The Flatlanders : now it's now again / by John T. Davis.
      pages cm — (American music series)
  Includes discography.
  ISBN 978-0-292-74554-4 (paperback : alkaline paper)
1. Flatlanders (Musical group) 2. Country music groups—Texas—
Lubbock. I. Title. II. Series: American music series (Austin, Tex.)
  ML421.F558D38 2014
  781.642092'2—dc23

                                        2014010702

doi:10.7560/745544

Old photographs turn yellow
Times they come and go
We can still do the boogie
From the High Plains to Mexico
Some old angel from Amarillo
Must be helpin' us to hold it on the road

"Flatland Boogie"
TERRY ALLEN

This book is for Kathy, from whom all good things flow . . .
and for Marcos Cordova, a good man.

Contents

Acknowledgments

Joe, Butch, Jimmie, Steve, Tony, Lloyd . . . Sharon, Adrienne, Janet . . . and all the more than three dozen men and women who shared their time, insight, and stories with me in the preparation of this volume.

Casey Kittrell and the good folks at U.T. Press, including copyeditor Paul Spragens and book designer Lindsay Starr.

Peter Blackstock and *No Depression*.

Cameron and Peter and New West Records.

The two Lances—Lance Cowan and Lance Webb.

Two books were most helpful for quotes and in researching this volume: Joe Carr and Alan Munde's *Prairie Nights to Neon Lights* (Texas Tech University Press, 1995), a history of West Texas music; and Christopher Oglesby's *Fire in the Water, Earth in the Air* (University of Texas Press, 2006), an oral history of West Texas musicians (along with Chris's website, www.virtua lubbock.com/).

Another valuable source for background and quotes was Amy Maner and George Sledge's 2005 documentary film, *Lubbock Lights*.

David Brown of KUTX-FM in Austin.

Michael Ventura and the poets, philosophers, and seekers on 14th Street.

And a tip of the Stetson to Miles Arceneaux, my favorite Famous Arthur.

Introduction

I'll concede the point—most books about contemporary musical groups do not start off with depictions of Plains Indians and tales of Spanish conquistadores journeying over a vast sea of grass.

But the Flatlanders—Joe Ely, Jimmie Dale Gilmore, Butch Hancock, Steve Wesson, Tony Pearson, and in lesser roles, Tommy X. Hancock and the late Sylvester Rice—are not just any band of musicians. Not only are Ely, Gilmore, and Hancock distinguished songwriters on their own, but the band they formed had a seminal influence on many of the roots/Americana/singer-songwriter inheritors that permeate contemporary music.

Musically, they came of age when Bob Dylan released his country-tinctured albums *John Wesley Harding* and *Nashville Skyline*, both recorded in Music City, while his former bandmates, The Band, holed up in a pink house in Woodstock to put their own spin on old wine in new bottles. In Los Angeles, Gram Parsons, the Flying Burrito Bros., and the Byrds were performing a shotgun wedding of rock and old-school country, tipping their hats to the Beatles and Buck Owens simultaneously.

But the Flatlanders didn't hail from L.A., New York, or Nashville. They arose in the isolation of what wannabe sophisticates derisively call "flyover country," and the diverse influences they absorbed and the natural and intellectual forces that shaped them made them unique and unquantifiable. And, God knows, folks have tried to quantify them over the years.

Just as their music is beyond category, the region they hail from is not just any ordinary landscape.

If the tale of the Flatlanders is to be properly told, it has to start with the circle of earth and sky that shaped them in the beginning and that still informs their music and worldview.

And it has to start with Lubbock, Texas, the insular, isolated, deeply conservative, deeply religious town that produced (and continues to produce) an improbable number of artistic and intellectual mavericks.

So . . . indulge a few historic and geographic digressions. It will all make sense, honest.

Lubbock and its surroundings are a region and a subject matter that cut close to my bones. I come from four generations of Lubbock people, mostly teachers and builders and football coaches. My paternal grandparents' house, on 13th Street near Avenue Q, was an annual destination, and most of my closest and most enduring friends hail from the city.

As a general thing, my family members share the humble and honorable characteristics of most Hub City natives—they are friendly, honest, plainspoken, conservative, hardworking, self-reliant, and proud of their roots. Those are traits the Flatlanders and their own circle of West Texas friends share. Well, maybe not so much the "conservative" part.

One of the major league treats of a life spent in music journalism has been following and chronicling the careers of Joe Ely, Jimmie Dale Gilmore, and Butch Hancock.

As the rodeo cowboys say, "Let 'er buck!" I've had the pleasure of listening to Jimmie Gilmore charm a honky-tonk full of drunks with nothing more than his silvery, high-lonesome voice; I've floated through the desolate, jaw-dropping canyons of the Big Bend with Butch Hancock as our Rio Grande river guide, campfire balladeer, and trickster-coyote-in-residence; and I was in the audience as Ely and Bruce Springsteen—two of the greatest live performers of their generation—slugged it out toe-to-toe onstage in Austin. . . . Wonderful memories, indelible moments, never to be repeated.

I'm indebted for their friendship and generosity over the years to these three, as well as their warm and loving spouses—Sharon Ely, Janet Gilmore, and Adrienne Evans-Stark (soulful Texas women all and a book unto themselves)—and their remarkable children, a collective refutation to the cliché about talent skipping a generation.

This book is about them, but it's also for them. As our friends south of the Río Bravo say, *Él que por su gusto corre, nunca se cansa*. Who runs for pleasure never tires.

THE FLATLANDERS

PART ONE   *The Land*

*The flatter the land oh yes the flatter land but of course
the flatter the land and the sea is as flat as the land
oh yes the flatter the land the more yes the more
it has may have to do with the human mind.*

GERTRUDE STEIN

CHAPTER 1

The Llano

"The country is most barbarously large and final . . ."

Those words were penned by author Billy Lee Brammer as the opening sally in his political epic, *The Gay Place*. That book was set in a fictional Austin in the fifties and was meant to describe the rugged Hill Country surrounding the Texas capital.

But the phrase, with its hint of the primeval and untamed, might be better applied to the high, stark, prairie landscape some 250 miles northwest of Austin: the South Plains and the Llano Estacado. It is a country that inevitably informs the men and women in this book, and the music and art they make. How else to write about a group called the Flatlanders without beginning with the land itself?

Bracketed by the New Mexico mountain ranges to the west and the palisades of the Caprock tableland to the east, and stretching in an unbroken sweep up to Canada, the Llano and the Great Plains were nearly the last expanse of North America to be explored and settled.

People have lived on the Llano for thousands of years, though never, even now, in great numbers, and their hold on the land did and does seem tenuous. Lying entirely west of the 100th meridian, where annual rainfall drops below twenty inches and the lush East yields to the arid West, the plains were a landscape wholly foreign and intimidating to Anglo immigrants arriving from wetter, greener climes.

Native people—Clovis hunters, and the forefathers of the Kiowa, Cheyenne, Comanche, and Apache—drifted across the face of the Llano like cloud shadows. Barry Lopez, in his introduction to *Llano Estacado: An Island in the Sky*, writes about "the great reservoir of silence suspended above the plain, through which birdsong, wind-washed grass and thunder once flowed." Spirits dwelt in the land and in the sky, but everything else seemed elusive and transitory.

From any stationary perspective on the Llano, you stand in a circle of earth and sky divided by a distant and ruler-straight horizon.

"We often walked away from the town in the late afternoon sunset," recalled Georgia O'Keeffe, who taught art and painted in Canyon, near Amarillo, in 1917. "There were no paved roads and no fences—no trees—it was like the ocean but it was wide, wide land. . . . I had nothing but to walk into nowhere, and the wide sunset space."

When Coronado's Spanish conquistadores first entered the region in search of souls and plunder in 1541, they were awe-stricken, bordering on terrified.

S. C. Gwynne described the country as "a bad hallucination" in his Comanche history *Empire of the Summer Moon*, before going on to quote Coronado: "'Although I traveled over [the Plains] for more than 300 leagues, [there were] no more landmarks than if we had been swallowed up by the sea. . . . there was not a stone, nor a bit of rising ground, nor a tree, nor a shrub, nor anything to go by.'"

In popular lore, "Llano Estacado" is translated as the Staked Plains, the story being that Coronado and his men had to stab their lances into the featureless prairie to create a route back home. But some scholars take the phrase to mean "palisaded plains," referring to the ramparts of the Caprock formation, an outcropping running hundreds of miles and rising from two hundred to a thousand feet above the lower plains. The South Plains and the Llano have the Caprock as their eastern boundary.

As if the weird, spacey quality of the topography and the often malevolent weather—drought, apocalyptic thunderstorms, bone-chilling cold, tornados, dust storms, hail, and ceaseless, maddening wind—were not enough to retard the onset of Anglo settlement in the 1800s, there were the Comanches.

One of a plenitude of warring Plains Indian tribes, the Comanches vaulted to supremacy once they mastered warfare from atop horses they stole or captured from the Spanish. In their century-long heyday, their country, an enormous swath of Texas from just west of Austin to the uppermost regions of the Panhandle, was referred to simply as "Comancheria," and they guarded it with unparalleled ferocity.

"No tribe in the history of the Spanish, French, Mexican, Texan and American occupations of this land had ever caused so much havoc and death," wrote Gwynne. "None was even a close second."

It wasn't until 1874, when U.S. Army Col. Ranald Mackenzie broke the Comanches as a fighting force by invading their natural fortress at Palo Duro Canyon near present-day Amarillo and slaughtering their vast horse herd, that it was safe for Anglo settlement to move permanently onto the plains.

The army made the South Plains safe. The invention of the electric pump, which let dryland farmers tap the vast underground Ogallala Aquifer, as well as the opening of cattle trails, and later the railroads leading to markets in the north and east, made them profitable. The little towns, with their names so evocative of the strange, hard country—Levelland, Plainview, Sundown, Needmore, Brownfield, Grassland, Shallowater, Earth—began to take hold.

And at the center of the South Plains sat Lubbock.

CHAPTER 2

I would describe Lubbock as a great place to live.
But I wouldn't want to visit there.

TOMMY X. HANCOCK

The City

"In Lubbock," Butch Hancock likes to say, "you can see fifty miles in any direction. And if you stand on a tuna fish can, you can see a hundred miles."

Lubbock—home of the Texas Tech Red Raiders, white bread, and blue northers. The "Hub City" as boosters like to call it, alluding to the roads and railroad tracks that radiate out from the city like so many wagon wheel spokes.

It's such an ordinary little sand-scrubbed city, in the midst of so many miles of inelegant country, to be at the heart of so much mystery and lore.

Like a lot of towns on the plains, Lubbock feels arbitrary. You get the feeling that some westward-faring settlers were making their way to California when a wheel abruptly fell off the wagon.

"To hell with it," they seem to have said, and set up shop on the spot.

They weren't the first. The Lubbock Lake Landmark archaeological site on the north side of town documents a unique and unbroken eleven-thousand-year history of human settlement.

There are no obvious natural advantages to the location except for the thin stream of a branch of the Double Mountain Fork of the Brazos River. Atop the Caprock, on the edge of the Llano Estacado, exposed to the elements under a vast bowl of sky, Lubbock's earliest pioneers must have felt like they were becalmed at sea.

Ranchers and farmers who at last felt safe to venture out with their families into the former Comancheria founded the city in 1890.

Within a year, a newspaper was publishing, and Quakers, Baptists, and Methodists vied for the souls of the pious (including, one presumes, Catholic Tejano vaqueros and farmers). In the fall of 1909 the Santa Fe Railway reached town, the same year Lubbock incorporated as a city. The census next year counted 1,938 hardy denizens.

In 1923, the state legislature established Texas Technological College—Texas Tech, in modern parlance—and the town began to take on the trappings of a city. Dryland farming of cotton and sorghum boosted the fortunes of the isolated metropolis—it was the only handy mercantile center for banking, marketing, and wholesaling for hundreds of miles.

By 1950, when Ely, Gilmore, and Hancock were young boys, the Lubbock population stood at 71,747. (It was 229,573 by 2010, substantially larger than its two nearest neighbors, Amarillo and Midland.)

By 1980, there were some 250 churches in the city, one for every seven hundred residents, give or take.

Butch Hancock has observed wryly on numerous occasions, "Life in Lubbock taught me two things: One is that God loves you and he's gonna send you to Hell. The other is that sex is dirty and evil and nasty and filthy and sinful and bad and awful, and you should save it for the one you love."

Folks in Lubbock know what sin is, and they're ag'in' it.

As a consequence, wrote the late, great Molly Ivins, "The advantage of being able to identify sin is that you can go out and do it, and enjoy it. Lubbock gives people a lot to rebel against."

But, writing in *Texas Monthly* magazine, she also added, "In Lubbock, the world is about 88.3 percent sky. It takes a while to get used to, but after you do, Lubbock feels like freedom and everywhere else feels like jail."

In a town where salvation is a preoccupation, sin, by necessity, must be lurking around every corner. "There were lots of churches with signs and little slogans like 'LSD: Lust, Sin, Death,'" recalled Ely's drummer Davis McLarty to *Texas Monthly*. "I thought, 'Hmmmm, maybe I'll try it.'"

Lubbock was the largest dry city in the country until 1972, when liquor-by-the-drink was voted in so that folks could have a civilized cocktail in a bar or a restaurant. Before that, you could BYOB to a club and buy setups, seek out an after-hours joint in some cotton patch and drink with the police characters, join a private club (for a one-dollar "lifetime" membership), or patronize an obliging local bootlegger who smuggled in booze from wet precincts.

Liquor stores per se were confined to the Strip, a sort of mini-Vegas out on the Tahoka Highway, where the neon blared temptation on a first-name basis (Bob's, Cecil's, Doc's, Pinky's, etc.) and the honky-tonks thrived.

"They were all open seven nights a week with live bands," recalled steel guitarist and producer Lloyd Maines in the documentary film *Lubbock Lights*. "You could go across the city limits and get all the sin you wanted."

Alas, the Strip's heyday came to an end in 2009 when Lubbock voted to allow package stores in town.

There was a sort of unspoken social compact between people who might bump into each other on a beer joint dance floor on Saturday night and kneel side by side in the pew the next Sunday morning.

Writes Ivins, "Kent Hance, the former congressman from Lubbock, reports, 'When I was in college we went to the Cotton Club to dance, to pick up girls and to drink beer out of Coca-Cola cups in case a minister came in, and it would embarrass him and you both. Outside they had soap and water so you could wash that [cover-charge] stamp off your hand when you left at the end of the night, so it wouldn't show Sunday morning at church.'"

My own sainted mother, who migrated from heathen Louisiana to marry a Lubbock native, soon learned the drill: "Everybody was in church on Wednesday night and Sunday morning and if you weren't, everybody knew it."

In a 2013 theater presentation called *Is There Life after Lubbock?*, Joe Ely noted, "religion was having a heyday in the newly created [postwar] prosperity. The amount of sin brought about by the good times was directly proportional to the sinner's ability to tithe on a hungover Sunday morning."

Churches take up entire city blocks on Broadway's "Miracle Mile." Parking lots are vast seas of asphalt to accommodate the faithful. The First United Methodist Church boasts a twenty-six-foot rose window, one of the five largest in the world. In yo' face, Chartres Cathedral.

As socially and religiously conservative as Lubbock was and is, it was and is equally conservative when it comes to politics.

Conservatism in Lubbock didn't much resemble the Bob Taft/Eisenhower–style genteel big-city Republican variety; it was more of a flinty type of orthodoxy that was socially conservative and viewed most government above the local school board with the same narrow-eyed suspicion with which a rancher views a coyote. It was Tea Party country before there was ever such a thing. In Lubbock, the go-it-alone, rugged-individualist-against-the-frontier spirit was threaded through the city's DNA. And there is genuine merit in those pioneer values.

But the reality was more complex. Big Government played a large part in making life in the West possible.

The Morrill Land-Grant Act of 1862, for instance, enabled the sale of public land for the creation of land grant colleges in each state (Texas A&M and Prairie View A&M are the two beneficiaries in the state).

The Homestead Act carved out 160-acre farm sites and made them available for settlement to anyone willing to withstand the privations of the Western longitudes, while cheap federal water and agricultural subsidies made (and still make) irrigation farming not only possible, but profitable. It worked; the area today is the largest contiguous cotton-growing region in the world.

Federal grants of public land to railroad companies starting in the 1850s were designed both to expand rail coverage and to encourage westward migration and immigration. Four out of five transcontinental railroads were built with help from the federal government, and millions of acres of arable farm- and ranchland were opened up for settlement.

The array of New Deal legislation and agencies—the Rural Electrification Act, the Emergency Farm Mortgage Act, the Civilian Conservation Corps, the Works Progress Administration—helped take at least some of the sting out of the Depression in Dust Bowl–stricken West Texas.

But all this inconvenient history was as nothing against the conservative mind-set that prevailed in Lubbock and West

Texas through both Democratic and Republican eras of governance. It was an inherent contradiction that most in Lubbock never considered, let alone resolved.

One thing everyone could agree on, though, was this: Music was ubiquitous. Even the Sacred Harp shaped-note religious singers had their a cappella hymns. Everyone else played, or knew someone who did. Old-time "house parties" lasted all night. Little towns around Lubbock had Saturday night jamborees at which amateurs from fifty miles around would hasten to perform. The county-line honky-tonks and gin mills catered to the grown-ups.

Even people passing through were swept up. Johnny Hughes, who would go on to manage Joe Ely early in his career, told *Texas Monthly*, "All these Mexican migrant workers would come in to pick the cotton, and they just filled downtown on Sundays. They'd all come in from miles around. You had the accordions and *conjuntos*, and all the different things they brought with them."

Racial discrimination was a given in Lubbock, as it was in the rest of the state. Segregation was codified in law, and even after it wasn't it took a while for the city to accommodate itself to that fact; Lubbock schools were effectively segregated until a court order took effect in 1970. Praising God's universal compassion on the one hand while practicing Jim Crow racism on the other was not a hypocrisy unique to Lubbock, although given the civic emphasis on piety, the contrast looks especially glaring.

Politicians in West Texas in the 1950s talked as though the Red Menace was coming in on the next train. Sixty years later, in the 2012 presidential election, Republican Mitt Romney received nearly 70 percent of the county's votes versus Barack Obama's 29 percent; fully 71 percent of the voters voted a straight Republican ticket. Three months before the polls opened, a Lubbock County judge warned of violent civil unrest in the streets should Obama be reelected (he later claimed he had been taken out of context).

All of the aforementioned notwithstanding, people in Lubbock were and are, on the whole, friendly, forthright, self-reliant, live-and-let-live, plainspoken, and hardworking. Politics and religion are only part of the picture.

Texas Tech, especially its football program, is the glue that binds the town together. High-falutin' Big 12 conference rivals like Texas, Oklahoma, and Iowa State often get their asses handed to them when they come to the Red Raiders' house. Nothing else this side of dove-hunting season so unites the population.

Weather is the other universal denominator. No social interaction at any level of Lubbock society is complete without a discourse on the latest drought/flood/hailstorm/tornado/dust storm. If no fresh meteorological doom is threatening at the moment, old-timers will stand outside, hands in their hip pockets, look up at the pitiless sky, and mutter, "Wisht it'd go ahead and do somethin'."

"The weather can be meaner than a fourteen-year-old girl who realizes she'll never be homecoming queen," cracks playwright Jaston Williams in *Is There Life after Lubbock?*, adding, "Spring is the time of year that comes in like a lamb and goes out like an ax murderer."

In the late sixties and early seventies, when the Vietnam War—and opposition to it—were raging, Lubbock's small community of bohemians, would-be hippies, freethinkers, artists, and antiwar activists naturally banded together, as much out of self-defense and safety in numbers as shared sensibilities. Joe Ely recalled one time walking into the local Toddle House with long hair, ordering something to eat, and getting punched off his stool for his trouble.

Despite that, a small counterculture of the like-minded began to flourish underneath Lubbock's day-to-day radar.

"This whole community of friends spread out to be huge eventually," recalled Debby Savage, who was part of the circle.

"At the time, not many people wore their hair long or had the ideas we had. We were real curious and read like maniacs. We'd stay up all night reading and playing music and playing chess."

But that was later, after the seismic waves of the upheavals of the sixties made themselves felt even in far West Texas. In the early 1950s, Lubbock was a good place for returning World War II veterans like Jimmie Dale Gilmore's father, Brian, to raise a family.

Even then, there were occasional bits of weirdness to ruffle the societal fabric, like the "Lubbock Lights," the unexplained series of nighttime flyovers by mysterious circular lights for a couple of summer months in 1951 by . . . something. Speculation ran rampant: swamp gas, migrating birds (plovers were the popular suspect), some kind of Communist devilment, secret government experiments from White Sands gone awry. UFOs and Little Green Men. The local paper, the *Avalanche-Journal*, dubbed the phenomenon "Flying Whatsits."

The ubiquitous horizon has always inspired contradictory feelings. "It makes you feel like both that you're at the center of your own world and that you're one little ant in the middle of vast nothingness," said Joe Ely in *Lubbock Lights*. "You feel both insignificant, because there's nothing else, and you feel kind of like it's limitless."

"It was the largest town for nearly three hundred miles in any direction," echoed songwriter and visual artist Terry Allen in the film. "It was the center in that sense, but also like prison in that sense."

★ ★ ★

"They call Lubbock 'The Hub of the Plains.' The 'Plains' as op-
posed to the 'Fancies,'" said Jimmie Dale Gilmore playfully.
"I think it may be a euphemism for the middle of nowhere.
Lubbock is the fabled middle of nowhere. So to all of us,
everywhere else was somewhere."

From the notes of the Laguna Gloria Museum show
HONKY-TONK VISIONS, 1986

To a visitor, Lubbock can seem like a civic entity obsessed with
lines, grids, and order: The horizon-spanning rows of cotton,
the parallel tracks of the railroad lines that converge on the
town, the fenced-off rectangular pens of the cattle feedlots,
the white chalk lines of the football gridiron, the arrogant
angularity of a grain elevator or a wind turbine thrusting out
of the plains and into the sky. And there is, of course, that
distant, undifferentiated horizon line, so very distinct in the
high, dry air.

The red-brick streets in the older part of town are laid out
with right-angle pragmatism—the east/west streets are num-
bered, the north/south avenues are lettered. The Flatlanders
had their genesis at a rental house on the corner of 14th Street
and Avenue W. There's comfort in the uniformity.

On May 11, 1970, that uniformity was upset in a terrifying,
arbitrary instant. That night a monster tornado, three-quarters
of a mile wide, bearing winds of 250 mph, tore through the
heart of town, killed twenty-six, and did $135 million in damage
over a twenty-five-square-mile area, all in a matter of minutes.

With typical frontier spirit, the city picked itself up and
dusted itself off. New housing and commercial enterprises,
including a new civic center and airport, helped conceal the
storm's physical scars, but the Lubbock Tornado still lingers
in the memories of survivors and their offspring. Tornado

season, as much as football season and hunting season, has its place on the city's psychic calendar.

Even when tornados don't blow, there is the ceaseless wind. And the dust. Once, many years ago, the city's Chamber of Commerce or some such boosters launched a campaign of bumper stickers and magazine advertisements: "Welcome to . . . Lubbock . . . For All Reasons." A photographer behind the wheel of his car, who must have been laughing to keep from crying, caught a snapshot of a roadside billboard bearing the slogan, all but obscured by a curtain of blowing dust and tumbleweeds.

"Everything comes out of the air—the good and the bad," said Terry Allen. "Just the wind is enough really to drive you to music. You hear it whining through the weather stripping twenty-four hours a day for about six months and painting a picture is not gonna help. But I could sit down at an upright piano and make it stop. Just playing against the wind."

And yet, for a land and a city so relentlessly linear, much of the Lubbock landscape is defined by circles—some overt, some secret. There is the circle of the seasons, of course (sometimes it's cold and windy, sometimes hot and windy). There is Loop 289, which rings the city and is sliced into pie-shaped wedges by I-27 ("that hard-assed Amarillo highway," as Terry Allen sings), and U.S. 82 and U.S. 84.

There are the few ancient oval playa lakes that still endure, once oases for Indians and buffalo. From the air, the vast green circles of irrigated crops stand out like emerald bull's-eyes. Dancers in the honky-tonks still two-step in counterclockwise orbit (one school of thought holds that those Little Green Men in the Lubbock Lights were intrigued by the heat signatures from the revolving couples in the dance halls). Cars full of teenagers circled the Hi-D-Ho Drive-In like Indians around a wagon train.

Ely, Allen, and others remember the liberation that came with the automobile and how sometimes kids would park their cars in a circle, pointed inwards, out in the middle of a dark cotton field, all the car radios tuned to the same station (often the big clear-channel stations out of Mexico like XERF), and everyone would dance to the same song in the circle of criss-crossing headlights. A secret circle.

Circles—revolutions, evolutions, re-creations, and redis-coveries—are at the heart of the Flatlanders' story. Draw a straight line long enough and far enough and you encircle the earth. Although the West Texas horizon is a line, if you stand in the center of the landscape and turn 360 degrees, it's also a circle. Completion out of paradox.

Or, as Butch Hancock is fond of singing, "A circle in the sand is a work of art."

It is hard-bark country. "It has something to do with the violent emptiness," said musician Jon Dee Graham in *Lubbock Lights*. "It's not just flat and empty—it's the *flattest*, and it's the *emptiest*."

The boredom engendered by the flatness, the emptiness, the dust, and the wind could be eye-glazing. You had to make your own fun, and some of it was potentially mortal; friends of mine would jump between moving boxcars just to feel alive.

One guy of Ely's acquaintance rigged up a car so he could drive it from the backseat to freak out the cops. One kid's daddy owned a dry cleaner, and the boy would open up the back after hours so his buddies could try on everyone's clothes. It was all about making your own fun, or going crazy. Or both.

"At night the city was ours because it all closed down," recalled songwriter Jo Carol Pierce, who was Jimmie Dale Gilmore's high-school sweetheart (and first wife). "We lived in alleys during the night."

Terry Allen used to show up at the doorstep of his own sweetheart's house, ostensibly for a date, and announce, with no preamble, "Run for your life!" The pair would scramble through the deserted nighttime streets and back alleys and parking lots all night long. Pursued or pursuing? It hardly mattered. They'd arrive back before dawn, huffing and puffing and grinning like fools. "Whew! We made it!"

As a girl, Sharon Thompson (later Sharon Ely) practiced what she called Disaster Gypsy Fashion, laying out her nicest dresses during tornado season just in case she met a cute boy in a storm shelter. Once, she created a series of life-sized dolls to keep her company during a period when all her friends had moved away. That sounds like it ought to be a maudlin story, but it's more endearing than anything else when she tells it.

The title of a 1984 Texas Tech museum show commemorating seventy-five years of musical history in West Texas summed up the prevailing gestalt precisely: the show was called *Nothin' Else to Do*. The phrase would go on to become something of a Flatlanders leitmotif.

But that was then. The city has moved on and changed and mellowed in the six decades since the Flatlanders grew up there. There is actually a respectable urban canopy, for one thing: Trees! Mixed-race couples no longer turn heads on the sidewalks. Texas Tech, thanks in part to a robust research program, is one of the top schools in the Southwest. The Internet and satellite TV have obliterated the cultural isolation that was once so confining. There are kosher sections in the groceries, and one can pray at a local mosque, if so inclined. And, as writer (and Lubbock resident) Michael Ventura noted, the once-ubiquitous Texas twang has moderated itself into "San Fernando Valley with a lilt."

Though Ely, Hancock, and Gilmore are long gone, gifted musicians like Amanda Shires, Cary Swinney, and Charlie Shafter continue to emerge from the Hub City.

But back in the 1950s if you ran a cotton gin or were an elder in the Church of Christ or a home-ec teacher at Monterey High, or held down the loan desk at the locally owned bank or ran the Kiwanis Club, or were, in short, one of the solid, respectable, conservative, middle-class Anglo bricks in Lubbock's wall of complacency, you might be forgiven for thinking that God was in his Heaven and all was right (barring the occasional tornado) in West Texas.

In the mid-1950s, when the Flatlanders were boys, Lubbock seemed far removed from the societal rumblings, race riots, and recessions of distant big-city headlines. The city and its citizens seemed destined to spend the Eisenhower years in placid, measured isolation.

Well . . . as John Wayne's character famously remarked in 1956's *The Searchers*—"That'll be the day."

CHAPTER 3

The Invasion

"Rock 'n' roll," recalled Terry Allen, "hit Lubbock like a bomb."

Allen, who was born in Wichita, Kansas, but whose parents got him to Amarillo and then Lubbock as fast as they could, had a ringside seat to the explosion. His father, Fletcher Manson "Sled" Allen, a former pro ballplayer for the St. Louis Browns, opened Sled Allen's Jamboree Hall, a multiuse venue on Texas Avenue that booked, among other things, a segregated bill of rhythm-and-blues acts on Friday and country-and-western stars on Saturday. Young Terry worked the aisles, selling soda pop to the kids and setups to the grown-ups with a half-pint hidden in their boot.

He recalled the avid sense of possession with which kids greeted those first hits by Elvis, Little Richard, Jerry Lee Lewis, Bo Diddley, and the rest of the invading barbarians. For many of them, this was the first thing in their lives that didn't come down through an adult filter.

Allen said, "'Blue Suede Shoes' had such a major impact on me because it was one of the first songs I was conscious of that didn't address your parents or your church or your school or any institutions—it was aimed right at you."

It's hard to overstate the impact that rock 'n' roll had on kids in West Texas. Radio shows like the *Louisiana Hayride* and the *Big D Jamboree* featured rock and rockabilly stars, and the Mexican clear-channel stations beamed blues and rhythm-and-blues musicians like Jimmy Reed, Muddy Waters, and Chuck Berry across El Norte. As a consequence, teenage bands sprang up across the South Plains like spring wildflowers.

But perhaps more than anything else, it was Elvis Presley who jump-started rock 'n' roll in West Texas. Just a few months after his string of hits on Sun Records commenced, Presley was barnstorming West Texas, making multiple appearances in Lubbock, Midland/Odessa, and Amarillo starting in January of 1955.

Sonny Curtis, who would go on to play with Buddy Holly's Crickets and write hits as diverse as "I Fought the Law" and the theme to the *Mary Tyler Moore Show*, recalled Presley's impact: The singer was wearing a red jacket, orange pants, and white buck shoes. "He looked like a motorcycle headlight coming at you," Curtis told author Christopher Oglesby.

Jimmy Bowen, who played with Buddy Knox and later became head of Capitol Records Nashville, saw Elvis in Amarillo along with Knox. "He wrecked the place," Bowen added to Curtis's account. "The girls were tearing at his clothing, and we thought, 'This is for us!'"

The grown-ups were busy two-stepping to West Texas country stars like Hoyle Nix and Tommy Hancock's Roadside Playboys—as far as they were concerned, Elvis could have stepped right off of one of the Lubbock Lights. But their kids latched onto Presley like he was long-lost kinfolk. He was the

Hillbilly Cat, their parents for the most part hated him, and he was all theirs.

A very young Jimmie Dale Gilmore went with his dad (who happened to play electric guitar himself) to see Presley and Johnny Cash on a package show at the South Plains Fairground Coliseum. The experience was beyond eye-opening.

"That was a bombshell!" the future Flatlander enthused more than half a century later.

"I remember it was louder than anything else I'd ever heard," he said. "Johnny Cash was rocking as much as Elvis was. And it was *fun!*"

(Down in Houston, songwriter Rodney Crowell had a similar reaction when he first saw Cash, Carl Perkins, and Jerry Lee onstage together: "Six years old and just barely off my daddy's knee / When those rockabilly rebels sent the Devil running right through me.")

It wasn't as though music were a foreign language or an exotic concept in Lubbock. Far from it. It was and is shared and passed down as a common vocabulary. As the saying goes, it's in the wind.

Maybe air-conditioning—or lack thereof—had something to do with it. On stifling summer nights, parents and offspring retreated to the porch, where the guitars and mandolins and fiddles were tuned up.

"Every other house had a piano or a fiddle or a guitar, and somebody who knew how to play it," Waylon Jennings told *Texas Monthly*. Jennings grew up in Littlefield, just northwest of Lubbock. "Music was the only thing we had."

"At the time [growing up] it just seemed fun and normal," said the Dixie Chicks' singer Natalie Maines in *Lubbock Lights*, speaking of making music around the house. "I didn't know that other people weren't doing the exact same thing. I didn't know that other people's families couldn't pick up the guitar and every other instrument and have sing-alongs and things like that." The Maines' professional music pedigree, it should be noted, goes back three generations.

The wind blew music in, but the musicians stirred it up. People in West Texas didn't get their music delivered to them already codified into arrangements, rigid genres, and stylistic compartments, courtesy of the big shots in New York, L.A., and Nashville. In the Panhandle outback, they took bits and pieces of what were at hand and what they liked and mashed it all together like refried beans.

Bob Wills, for example, did not invent Western Swing. But he took it to a national audience by mixing elements of Dixieland jazz, Texas string bands, cowboy songs, razzmatazz inspired by old-time minstrel shows, Big Band vocals, pop stylings, hot country fiddle licks, and a jazzman's passion for improvisation.

Music had always been a riposte to the intimidating silence of the plains, going back to the cowboy songs collected by John A. Lomax. The ubiquitous church choir, the all-night house parties, the county-line honky-tonks, and the school marching band all provided their own soundtracks. Families listened to the radio shows of the day. And every now and then a turtle-backed Flixible touring bus would roll up to the Jamboree Hall or the Cotton Club and disgorge Ernest Tubb or Ray Price or Hank Snow.

Elvis was a big stone tossed into a West Texas musical stock tank. The ripples and reverberations spread outward and began to reflect back.

In Wink, out in the Permian Basin oil patch, there were the Teen Kings, featuring a young man with a remarkable four-octave range named Roy Orbison. Buddy Knox, of "Party Doll" fame, blew out of Canyon, a tiny burg near Amarillo, with his wonderfully named band, the Rhythm Orchids. Knox's band for a while featured a wet-behind-the-ears sax player from Slaton named Bobby Keys, who would go on to play for both Joe Ely and the Rolling Stones. As Keys told journalist Robert Greenfield, going on the road with a band in the fifties "beat the shit out of Pony League baseball and the Methodist Youth Fellowship."

There were a hundred one-hit wonders like Johnny "Peanuts" Wilson, who recorded a subversive hit called "Cast-Iron Arm," and the Legendary Stardust Cowboy (aka Norman Odam), who made it all the way to national TV's hit show *Laugh-In*. But for the merest circumstance of luck and timing, Ely, Gilmore, and Hancock might have been among them, rumors in their own time.

The first impulse of a lot of kids across West Texas in the wake of Elvis's invasion was to pick up a guitar if they didn't have one already. It was a natural reaction and an easy transition. The country music being made in the dance halls in the South Plains and the Panhandle was already a kissing cousin to rockabilly and early rock 'n' roll.

The de facto purpose of music in that place and that era was to put people on the dance floor and keep 'em there. Even today, bands from elsewhere can get spooked when they play for crowds in West Texas and no one applauds; the way you know you're getting over is if people dance.

That being the case, there was a strong emphasis on the beat, a driving rhythm on the up-tempo numbers and an instrumental interplay among, for instance, the rhythm guitar, steel guitar, and fiddle. Drums were essential in the noisy confines of your average roadhouse, and pedal steel and electric guitars that could punch through the clamor were getting more common in the early fifties.

So the building blocks for rock 'n' roll were already in place when Lubbock kids began melding those elements with the blues and R&B influences they heard on the big Mexican stations and the late-night grooves of Bo Diddley, Little Richard, and Ray Charles via stations like KWKH out of Shreveport.

And one of those local kids was named Charles Hardin "Buddy" Holley.

Buddy Holly (his last name on his first record contract was a misspelling, and it stuck), he of the heavy-rimmed glasses, Stratocaster guitar, and hiccupping vocals, is the still the Polaris of modern music in West Texas. But he was much more than that.

His influence on rock 'n' roll is vast and immutable. Born in Lubbock on September 7, 1936, Holly not only left his stamp on American music, but on pop music worldwide. Four kids in Liverpool, England, growing up in circumstances every bit as grim as any Lubbock had to offer, took their instrumentation, approach to songwriting, and even their name—the Beatles—from Holly and his band, the Crickets.

The big shadow Holly cast has been amply documented. He and his band—which at times included Sonny Curtis, Jerry Allison, Joe B. Mauldin, Don Guess, Niki Sullivan, Larry Welborn, Tommy Allsup, and (on Holly's last, ill-fated tour) Waylon Jennings—went on to influence not only the Beatles, but also the Rolling Stones, Bob Dylan, Bruce Springsteen, and myriad others.

Holly and the Crickets codified the classic rock 'n' roll lineup—lead guitar, rhythm guitar, bass and drums, and a lead vocalist. He was a trailblazer in recording his own material and using his own band in the studio in an era when producers routinely selected material for their artists to record, and professional studio sidemen supplanted a band's musicians.

Holly pioneered the use of overdubs in recording and by the end of his life was experimenting with sophisticated orchestral pop arrangements and studio effects. He was, literally, ahead of his time. The critic Don McLeese described his innovative sound as a "rock 'n' roll synthesis of country roots and rhythm-and-blues grit with a twist of Texas twang."

And his appeal was international. To British fans, he was what the Beatles would become to Americans—a massive attraction and an ambassador of pop culture.

His career, as successful and far-reaching as it was, was heartbreaking in its brevity. From his first release, "That'll Be the Day" (the title lifted from John Wayne's signature line in *The Searchers*), through hits like "Oh Boy," "Peggy Sue," "Not Fade Away," "Rave On," "It's So Easy," and more, Holly's meteoric career lasted only a shade over eighteen months. His death, in a plane crash in a snowy Iowa field on February 3, 1959, came when he was just twenty-two.

Fans, particularly from the U.K., made annual pilgrimages to leave guitar picks and sheet music on Holly's grave in Lubbock, but the city at large never embraced him, at least until it figured out there was a buck to be made off the hometown-boy-made-good.

Don McLean's chart-topping 1971 hit, "American Pie," helped bring Holly back into the public consciousness, citing his death as "the day the music died." The 1978 movie *The Buddy Holly Story* was a heavily fictionalized pastiche (mountains in Lubbock!), but Gary Busey's riveting, Oscar-nominated, heartfelt performance as Holly captured the spirit of the man.

It took Lubbock a long time to get with the program. There was a Buddy Holly Park, it's true, but for years live music was banned there because fans might trample the turf. The irony was lost on no one except the city's leaders.

Finally, in 1980, the city unveiled a bronze statue of Holly by Western sculptor Grant Speed. An adjacent West Texas Walk of Fame was begun in 1983 (both since relocated to the downtown Buddy Holly Center).

In 1999, the city established the Buddy Holly Center, which preserves, collects, and promotes the legacy of Holly and West Texas music and musicians. Today, the city hosts an annual Lubbock Music Fest, which is part homage to Holly and often features members of the Crickets.

Lubbock civic leaders were for many years myopic with regard to Holly's influence and his impact on West Texas music. But to the Flatlanders they were immediate and profound.

Joe Ely, who may be the closest thing Holly has to a musical heir, is still in awe of what Holly created, working in a virtual vacuum.

"The thing that blows me away is listening to his melodies," Ely said. "And wondering. Here's this guy, he didn't have a lot of resources in Lubbock. There weren't a lot of things he could have possibly drawn from in the early fifties, when he was first learning to play. I'm always amazed at how he could have come up with the melodies he did."

"It was almost like they came to him from some other place," he told the *Austin American-Statesman*. "Roy Orbison was the same way, with those really haunting melodies, and for both of those guys to grow up pretty much at the same time, less than 100 miles from each other, almost scared me to death when I thought about it too hard."

At the same time, Holly was graspable to Lubbock youth in a way that the otherworldly Elvis was not. Here was a gangling, four-eyed kid who spoke with a West Texas twang and who had just a few years earlier been walking beside them down the halls of Lubbock High. Now, seemingly overnight, that same skinny kid was topping the record charts and appearing on *American Bandstand* and the *Ed Sullivan Show*. Holly had *done* it, and done it from Lubbock! Maybe they could do it, too.

There were little small-town coincidences that in hindsight seemed to augur bigger things. Lawrence Holley, Buddy's dad,

bankrolled Jimmie Dale Gilmore's first demo recording sessions. Butch Hancock grew up across from the Holleys' house,
although they had moved on by then. And one day a traveling
salesman showed up at Joe Ely's parents' house peddling steel
guitar lessons. It turned out he worked for the same company
that had tutored Buddy as well.

Buddy Holly showed what was possible, and he spun gold
out of the disparate styles of music coexisting in West Texas. It
was left to the next generation of Lubbock musicians to blaze
paths that even Holly himself never imagined.

CHAPTER 4

And the stars fell on 14th Street
I was livin' with some friends of mine
And the night sky burned in the city heat
But the fire must have been in our minds

"14th Street"
BUTCH HANCOCK

The House

There was this house. It still sits on the northwest corner of 14th Street and Avenue W. It isn't much to look at: A one-story brick Craftsman-type bungalow, built in the late twenties, with muddy brown trim and a small porte cochere, typical of mass-market prewar design. An expansive front porch. Bare lawn, a few scraggly trees. A look of hard use and neglect.

The house is in what used to be called affectionately the "Tech Ghetto." It was an older area just east of the Texas Tech campus full of low-cost rental properties—small houses and garage apartments—that were attractive to students on a budget.

Only a fragment of the Tech Ghetto remains today. The notorious 1970 tornado turned part of it into a tossed salad, and most of the remainder was bulldozed for newer and more expensive condo/apartment and retail developments and a crosstown highway.

Yet the house on 14th Street, improbably, remains. It is located, technically, in the South Overton residential district, which is listed in the National Register of Historic Places. If Lubbock had a properly developed sense of artistic commemoration, it would slap a historical plaque of its own on the place.

★ ★ ★

Remember how we used to be here now
Livin' in the moment
For days and days and nights and days on end

"Now Is Now Again"
THE FLATLANDERS

———

It was at that house, in the late sixties and early seventies, that a nucleus of young men and women began to congregate. It was in that house, more than anywhere else, that the Flatlanders had their genesis.

But the Flatlanders, as a group, were almost an afterthought. They were just one small subcomponent of a group of *compañeros* bound together as much by an unquenchable thirst for new ideas and the thrill of shared experience as by music or any kind of artistic vision. "We didn't have to agree, but we did have to explore," remembered one of the principals. The folks who lived in, dropped by, and hung out at the 14th Street house were on a voyage of self-discovery.

That last sentence looks overbearing and pompous on the page, but consider the context. If in the late sixties in Lubbock you were a young draft-age male with long hair and an inquiring mind, or if you were a young woman with her own ideas about sexual autonomy and gender roles, you dwelt mainly in isolation. Kindred maverick spirits were few and far between. Those who found one another were thrilled by the shared sense of recognition. *Thank Gawd I'm not the only one!*

"It was a group of friends that grew and grew, and most weren't musicians," said Jimmie Dale Gilmore. "There were all these different circles that came together. They were all music lovers, so the musicians amongst the group were revered. But there were also artists and writers and [Tech] professors.

"That group was the incubator that made the Flatlanders. I see the history as being the history of that group, rather than just the Flatlanders. I think it's important to bring that out."

Michael Ventura is an author, essayist, and poet, a street-smart Yankee with a formidably catholic intellect. He literally dropped into the 14th Street scene right after New Year's 1973, in the wake of a snowstorm, hitching a ride en route from Santa Cruz to Nashville. He was amazed by what he found.

"I walked in and there were these gorgeous women—Sharon Thompson, Laura Hunt, Debby Savage—and I was stunned. The other thing that stunned me was a library of books in the house I'd never seen before—Sufi texts, Krishnamurti—way before that stuff started hitting the West Coast.

"In New York, I could go into any bookstore and get any book of poetry I wanted. Here, it was a *real* different thing when somebody handed somebody a copy of Ginsberg."

"It was a group of highly creative people who also felt stultified by Lubbock," continued Jimmie. "They were rebellious, but not destructive or hostile. Experimental kinds of people. It was like huddling together for warmth in such a repressive kind of atmosphere."

"All of us except Butch came from families that had broken aspects," said Janette Norman, who had been Butch's sweetheart before and through the 14th Street days.

"Somebody brought a picture of a group of little monkeys clinging together in a cage and set it on the mantle. You could see the terror, but also see the love. Joe said, 'That's us—those little monkeys holding onto each other. We'll do anything for each other.'"

Butch Hancock summed up the prevailing vibe with typical haiku-like efficiency: "It was one of those houses where there was always somebody asleep and there was always somebody awake."

When the weather permitted, they'd play guitars on the roof. Often they'd sleep up there, too, to be awakened by the gas meter reader or the mailman.

"We kept no recognizable hours," Butch recalled.

There wasn't much recognizable income, either. When the landlord came around to collect the eighty-dollars-a-month rent, the half dozen or so permanent residents sometimes had to hide in the cellar (thus dodging their thirteen-dollars-per-head monthly tab). No one seems to recall there ever being a front door key.

Sex, drugs, and rock 'n' roll? Not so much. For one thing, no one could finance any debauchery worthy of the name.

"We couldn't afford it!" laughed Joe Ely. "We never had any money, but we never needed any. Everybody always had just enough for a bag of rice or a couple of potatoes. And our whole entertainment was entertaining ourselves."

Laura Hunt and Tony Pearson (the Flatlanders' future mandolin player) opened a health food store—a quixotic enterprise in Lubbock in those days—so there was a supply of beans and granola and other hippie chow to be had. Laura and Tony called their enterprise the Supernatural Health Food Store. When the Flatlanders began playing "real" gigs, they at first christened themselves the Supernatural Playboys.

People paired off, of course. Butch and Janette. Joe and Sharon were always an item. Debby Savage eventually became Jimmie's second wife.

Mostly, as the participants recall it, it was relatively friction-free. Which is not to say that life on 14th Street was an effortless, idle hang.

"It wasn't tranquil," asserted Ventura. "There was a terrific sense of intensity and a kind of intimacy. There were jealousies, there were envies, there was 'who's the smartest guy and who's the prettiest girl.' But there was intense artistic and intellectual excitement."

Butch and Jimmie had begun to dip their toes into the songwriting pool, and they began to debut their own songs at the all-night picking parties around the big slab of a wooden coffee table in the living room that Butch had crafted from a door. If Joe was penning songs at the time, he kept them, for the moment, to himself.

One night, Jimmie might debut, say, "Down in My Hometown," and the next night Butch might return the volley with a new song of his own like "Stars in My Life." In between, they'd play the scores, if not hundreds, of songs they knew in common: folk, blues, country, pop, cowboy songs, Cajun waltzes, you name it.

"Butch was a little bit . . . Butch seemed a little bit veiled. He was more mysterious than some of the others," said Cynthia Spanhel, one of the women who frequented the scene. "But not more [mysterious] than Joe. Joe always seemed a little more unapproachable. His emotional life was worked out through his music." But Jimmie, she said, "was always easy to know."

"Jimmie enjoyed being the teacher," Janette wrote me in an e-mail. "And he was and is a ravenous student. Joe was our practical problem solver—fixer, rigger. He gets things done without hesitation. Butch was expansive and disciplined. Intensely observant and challenges himself."

"We were just a bunch of girls and guys hanging out and having the greatest time," said Sharon Ely. "Those living room concerts were incredible music."

The women at 14th Street played roles of their own, some traditionally supportive, some harder to define.

Sharon was the ringleader. "Her energy levels whirled like a West Texas tornado," said Norman. She lived in the dining room and always seemed to have a pot of posole or beans going on the stove.

"We prayed before every meal," recalled Janette. "Sometimes they were gratitude prayers, sometimes they were celebration prayers, sometimes they were the funniest prayers you could imagine. But they were always a celebration of who we were."

"We made every occasion special," recalled Deborah Milosevich, aka "Big Deb," one of the regulars. "Sharon was in charge of that. It could be anything—a full moon—and it would be an occasion to pull the swimming pool out on the roof and get the champagne and cheesecake out."

"We were a bunch of misfits and when we finally found each other, we just bonded and it was our family," said Debby Savage, aka "Little Deb." "And it was family to such an extent that there was an unspoken agreement that we accepted each other unconditionally."

They were, she said, "very moral for the time and the kind of lifestyle we had." There was, of course, the round-robin dating common to close groups. Big Deb dated Steve Wesson for a good while; Little Deb became Jimmie's second wife; Laura Hunt dated Jimmie and then Steve, and so on. But the group was the group. Once, when the guys were playing in a corner of Texas Tech, the women banded together and swept the campus to round up an audience.

"Ventura says those guys were writing those songs for us," said Milosevich, who went on to become an acclaimed sculptor.

"It's hard to describe, because it wasn't just a bunch of girls hanging around a bunch of musicians. It was deeper than that. The girls were really good friends. The best I can say is that it felt like we were all in love with each other. We really appreciated each other's gifts. We still stay in touch with one another."

It was avant-garde in its way, but it was still Lubbock, and still West Texas. And the roles of the day were still the roles of the day.

Jo Carol Pierce, looking back on those days, told the *New York Times* in 1993, "It was the most traditional scene you could imagine, even when we were being hippies. It was the women in the kitchen talking about vitamins and the men out playing music. That was before *Ms.* magazine or anything."

"We were hanging around cooking healthy food and dancing and being some of the best fans they had at the time," Sharon recalled.

"She was a great cook, so she fit right in," said Steve Wesson of Sharon.

Overt feminists or no (and in their various left-of-center ways, they were groundbreaking in that regard), the women of 14th Street were, asserted Sharon, "an integral part of the Flatlanders."

One night in 1970, Butch, Jimmie, and Joe found themselves in Butch and Janette's living room on 10th Street, playing together (as far as Jimmie recalls) for the first time.

Butch rolled out a couple of originals, and the trio shared a few standards they knew in common, and then Jimmie volunteered a jokey B-side from a Ray Price record whose lyrics ran, in their entirety: "This is the shortest song in the world."

Suddenly, everyone caught the express train to Goofball City. As journalist Don McLeese recounted in the *Statesman*, "In the midst of gales of laughter, they committed themselves to performing what would be the longest song in the world, the slowest of slow blues, with the three alternating lines like 'This is the looongest, just about the l-o-o-o-n-g-e-s-t . . .' An hour or so into this, some friends started yawning, others leaving, while the three remained oblivious to anything beyond this extended exercise in musical extremism.

"'That kind of sealed our fates forever,' said Gilmore. 'We realized all three of us were insane enough to do that. . . . There was something over-the-edge about all three of us.'"

What is impressive in hindsight is not that these young men—in 1970, Butch and Jimmie were twenty-five and Joe was twenty-three—were writing their own songs, but that those songs were so lyrically sophisticated,

Butch's "One Road More" is shot thorough with wry humor ("Lord, I ain't got a lick of sense, I got a crazy mind / Cause I don't want to leave and I don't want to stay behind").

Jimmie's "Tonight I Think I'm Gonna Go Downtown," by contrast, is a long, yearning existential ache ("I told my love a thousand times / That I can't say what's on my mind / But she would never see / This world's just not real to me").

Juxtapose that to Butch's "Shadow of the Moon," a love song that is almost giddy with anticipation ("It might take a lifetime, darlin', or it might take a day / When our crossroads come together the stars will shine and the band will play / When I cross your lifeline, darlin', we'll sing a happy tune / The river will roll and turn to gold in the shadow of the moon").

To which Jimmie responded with "Dallas," perhaps his best-known song and a song that contains one of the most effortlessly evocative opening lines in modern music: "Have you ever seen Dallas from a DC-9 at night?" Decades from now, when we're all flying around in *Jetsons*-style rocket pods, Jimmie's beautiful, alliterative image of a vintage 1960s twin-engine jet banking low over the Trinity River and the red neon Pegasus sculpture beaming out from Big D's skyline will remain timeless and resonant.

So here came these songs and many more, unfiltered through the transitory pop fashions of the day (emerging from what Butch called "a crude innocence"), spilling out around living rooms and front porches and impromptu jam sessions, night after night. It was exhilarating, and liberating.

Even the animals in residence at 14th Street seemed tuned in to some otherworldly frequency.

"There was a dog there, a little chow dog named Pebbles, who was a psychic dog," recalled Butch. "He had the surrounding three or four blocks completely intimidated. He'd be lying asleep back in the bathroom on the cool linoleum and all of a sudden he'd go zooming out, crashing through the screen door and run a block away and bite somebody on a bicycle. Some innocent guy that didn't have the right vibes or something."

And there were funny little moments of serendipity that seemed emblematic of that charmed time and place.

One day in 1968 Ely was driving out to the Strip when he saw a fellow with a backpack and a guitar hitchhiking by the side of the road.

"He was completely in the wrong place to catch a ride," he remembered. "I kind of associated with him because I'd been doing some of that myself, so I just kind of pulled over. He was going down to Austin or Houston, so I took him out to where he could get a good ride."

By way of thanks, the stranger reached into his knapsack and pulled out a record album—that's all the pack contained, copies of the same record. No clothes, no toothbrush, no nothin'. Just records.

The hitchhiker's name was Townes Van Zandt. He had been in San Francisco recording his first album, *For the Sake of the Song*, and was hitchhiking home. Ely recalled thinking, "Wow, this is unusual; I'd never met anybody who'd actually made a record."

"Was it coincidence, or was it meant to be?" he wondered decades later in an NPR radio interview.

Ely took the album over to Jimmie Gilmore's house—because his dad had a turntable—and they promptly devoured it. Van Zandt was another Texas original, a left-of-center songwriting intellect. He would have fit in seamlessly at 14th Street.

"It became our favorite record," said Joe. "We learned 'Tecumseh Valley' immediately. I guess that record had a little bit to do with getting the Flatlanders together. I'm sure glad I stopped that day."

★　★　★

Where do we go from here?
Where do we make connections?
Sometimes I swear we were only born
Just to give and take directions

"Only Born"
BUTCH HANCOCK

———

"One of the distinctive characteristics of that music scene was that it was a huge tent," said Cynthia Spanhel, who recalled the era with affection. "All you had to do to be in it was to be interested in music. There would be big jam sessions [at the house], fifteen or twenty people, and they'd always end with 'Will the Circle Be Unbroken.'"

Ely, Gilmore, and Hancock might have been at the center of the 14th Street musical solar system, but there were plenty of other planets in the orbit as well.

One night a guy walked in the door carrying a saw. Sat down and commenced to play it with a mallet. Everyone agreed that was a hell of a thing.

The guy's name was Steve Wesson. He was from Dimmitt, a flyspeck northwest of Lubbock, and he was working as a technician in the Texas Tech art department while he finished his MFA. He'd ordered his musical saw from the *Whole Earth Catalog* and taught himself to play it, inspired by the use of a saw on old Jimmie Rodgers records. The eerie, keening notes of the saw (the pitch changed as the saw was bent) were sort of the equivalent of a chicken-fried theremin and served as a warbling counterpoint to the vocalists, particularly Jimmie Gilmore's reedy tenor.

Another regular was a cohort of Wesson's who served the same function Wesson did at Tech, but in the architecture department, which in those days adjoined the art department.

Tony Pearson and his wife had actually lived in the house on 14th Street previously, but he and his wife had moved out and, as Sharon put it, "We moved in."

After he and his wife divorced not long thereafter, Pearson didn't stay a stranger long; he found himself back at his old digs on many a night, adding his mandolin licks to the musical gumbo.

One of the final pieces of the Flatlanders puzzle never really fit in with the 14th Street crowd. Sylvester Rice was ten or fifteen years older, for one thing, and had a real job (or two), which also set him apart. Rice worked as a surveyor in a land office next to where Don Caldwell was putting together the pieces of what would become Lubbock's first dedicated recording studio. Rice found himself spending a lot of time hanging out there, and in turn meeting the musicians who wandered in. "He and Jimmie were particularly good friends," Butch recalled.

Then, too, he palled around with the local disc jockeys and concert promoters, learning the hustles and making connections. Some nights they would make the rounds, occasionally catching Ely and one of his early rock combos at the Koko Palace or the Town Pump. One of Rice's running buddies was a disc jockey on the local country station KDAV named Louis Driver, or "Country Lou D" (to distinguish him from disc jockey and TV host Lew Dee, at neighboring station KSEL).

Rice played stand-up bass with some local groups, including one band that included a popular local bandleader, Wilburn Roach. By one route or another, he too wound up sitting in with Butch, Joe, Jimmie, Tony, and Steve.

"I don't remember him at 14th Street," said Tony Pearson. "He played there a couple of times, maybe. Something needed some bass and he'd fill in. So he knew all the songs and everything."

Sylvester Rice wasn't the type to hang around with a bunch of hippies in a crash pad eating granola and sprouts. But he became a knocked-in-the-head fan of the music he heard them making.

And the day would come, not too far in the future, when he would play a pivotal role in moving the Flatlanders out of that house on 14th Street and into the wider world.

PART TWO

The Men,
First Verse

There was yet something boyish about him as he stood taking leave of the family. He stood in the frame that had always contained him, the great circular frame of the plains, with the wind blowing the grey hair at his temples and the whole of the Llano Estacado at his back. When he smiled at the children . . . he gave them the look that had always been his greatest appeal—the look of a man who saw life to the last as a youth sees it, and who sees in any youth all that he himself had been.

In a Narrow Grave
LARRY MCMURTRY

CHAPTER 5

Well, I left my home out on the great High Plains
Searching for some new terrain
Standing on the highway with my coffee cup
Wonderin' who's gonna pick me up

"I Had My Hopes Up High"
JOE ELY

Joe, Jimmie, and Butch, Part 1

Joe Ely is, no shit, the only guy I've ever known who really did run away and join the circus.

It was the spring of 1974, and Ely was briefly back in Lubbock after a prolonged period of rambling. Ely had been a vagabond since he dropped out of Monterey High School in his senior year. Prior to the formation of the Flatlanders, he'd bopped around from California to New York, Europe and back. The same horizon that spoke to Woody Guthrie, Jack Kerouac, John Steinbeck, and Henry Miller also beckoned to him. Life its ownself was out there, waiting to be savored. There were characters and stories and unexplored roads out there. And songs.

But anyway, the circus. Ely was back in town, restless, and here came the Ringling Bros. and Barnum & Bailey Circus. Michael Ventura put it concisely: "Elephants went through town, we were watching, and we followed the elephants. I was in love, so I stayed. He went away with it."

Ely caught on with Ringling Bros. and was put to work with the ring stock, the lowest spot on the circus totem pole. Before long, he was put in charge of managing the llamas and the World's Smallest Horse. Sixty bucks a week and all the cotton candy you could eat.

The llamas spit on him and the World's Smallest Horse took a bite out of his kneecap. "I hated that goddam horse," he recalled.

He stuck with it for about three months until Houston, where a runaway horse (who was emphatically *not* the World's Smallest) kicked him and caved some of his ribs in. He limped home to Lubbock with not much to show for the experience but some good stories and at least one new song called "Indian Cowboy."

It's hard to envision the guy who would become one of the most dynamic performers of his generation shoveling llama shit, but it was all grist for Ely's mill.

If one believes in predestination, then Joe Ely had no choice but to be a gypsy. He was born in 1947 in Amarillo, where his dad (like his grandfather) worked for the railroad. As a baby, Ely lived in a house that was midway between Route 66 and the BNSF switching yards. "As a kid," he recalled to England's *Dirty Linen* magazine, "I saw those trains being made up and disappearing out over the horizon and wondering where they went."

He had a primal memory of seeing Jerry Lee Lewis pound the piano during an outdoor performance in the midst of a vintage Panhandle dust storm at an Amarillo Pontiac dealership. It was a formative image, lodged in there with DNA-deep impressions of railroads and highways.

When Ely was twelve, his folks moved to Lubbock, where his father ran a downtown used-clothing store. Ely has fond memories of those days, when the migrant workers would swamp downtown during harvest and Mexican *conjuntos* and *corridos* punctuated the air. Joe learned Spanish and worked the register.

Like a lot of West Texas kids, music came to him early. He took violin lessons when he was eight and played in the school orchestra. One day, a door-to-door salesman offering steel guitar lessons knocked on the door. Ely recalls the amplifier the man was toting had a palm tree painted on the speaker grille. That was pretty cool. "That steel guitar sounded like what it looked like outside: dusty and windy," he recalled to *Texas Monthly*.

Many years later, he would learn that the same outfit the salesman worked for had given Buddy Holly guitar lessons.

Holly's influence was pervasive among Lubbock kids in those days. Before long, Joe discovered the Stratocaster, Holly's instrument of choice. "It was right after Buddy died," he remembered. "And there were a lot of twangy guitars around." The violin went on the closet shelf for keeps.

Ely's father died when he was thirteen, and his mother was briefly institutionalized shortly thereafter. Joe and his brother were farmed out to relatives. He helped bring in some extra money as a dishwasher and fry cook at a local greasy spoon called the Chicken Box.

Music was an antidote. "After my daddy died, and in the dreary days after that, that was when I first really got serious about playing music."

He never finished high school, despite making a spectacular debut on his first day as a freshman, riding a motorcycle down the halls of Monterey High.

He began putting bands together when he was thirteen. One of them, from his early high school days, was the Twi-Lites; a photo shows the five guys—kids, really—with Ely front and center, lounging on a bench and wearing matching baby blue cardigan sweaters and mock turtlenecks. The other guys' turtlenecks are white; Ely's is black. They opened for Ace Cannon and Jimmy Reed at the Koko Palace above the Koko Inn and even toured around the state and into Louisiana. "Whether prom, nightclub or private party," read their business card, "we will render the type of music most enjoyable."

As the group got more professional and started branching out, school took a backseat. "The nightclubs started hiring us, so I quit the day job," he said. Adios, Chicken Box. "Which, of course, annihilated my grades, but they were pretty much annihilated anyway," he told *Texas Monthly*.

In 1964, he quit high school and, as Mark Twain would say, lit out for the territories. Woody and Kerouac and Blind Lemon Jefferson were his spirit guides. "I just kind of followed in their footsteps," he said. "I'd hear the name of a town in a song and I'd go there. I don't know why."

One autumn, he and a buddy named Eddie Beethoven decided they'd hitchhike up to New England to see the fall colors. They hopped a freight train in Amarillo in short sleeve shirts and Levi jackets. By the time they finally made their convoluted way to the East Coast, the autumn leaves were long gone and winter was open for business. The two would-be tourists nearly froze to death. Ely played for street change on the sidewalks in lower Manhattan and slept on the Staten Island Ferry.

On another trip, Ely hitchhiked out to California and bought a beat-up guitar with clamshells glued to it from a junkie who needed speed worse than he needed a guitar. Ely wound up busking for change and sleeping on the beach in Venice with his Super Reverb amp as a pillow.

He came back, but he soured on the Hub City when the cops came knocking once too often.

"It was the very day that psilocybin and mescaline became illegal, and I was with a lady who was the head of the music department at Texas Tech," he recalled. "I was at her house with a bunch of kids and we were all eating mushrooms and about half of the Lubbock police force busted in and put us in jail."

A drug bust in Texas, in that era, was a serious beef. Dallas County grand juries had once been happy to hand down century-long sentences for possession of marijuana *seeds*.

Ely was sitting in the Lubbock County jug listening to Merle Haggard sing "Branded Man" on the radio. Not the ideal soundtrack. "They were threatening us with twenty years in jail because they wanted to make an example of us."

At the time, he said, "I never thought that I would actually go out and do something with music. Things were looking pretty bleak." As it turned out, he got probation. It was time to, as the song goes, put Lubbock in his rearview mirror.

"I moved to Austin and hooked up with Jim Franklin to go to New York City. I was going to help him mix paints for a mural he was doing."

It was around 1969 or '70, and via that connection with Austin artist Jim Franklin, who would go on to make the armadillo the ubiquitous Texas hippie mascot, Ely fell in with some expatriate radical U.T. theater students who were putting on a play called *Stomp* (not, it should be noted, the future Broadway hit of the same name). The play had caught the eye of famed producer Joseph Papp, who sponsored the group to come to NYC, and Ely became part of the troupe. He lived below a theater near Astor Place, among the dusty props, with the subway rumbling by on the other side of the wall.

When the company hopped overseas to Europe for some months, Ely jumped too. The kid in the powder-blue sweater ginning out cover hits with the Twi-Lites a few years earlier, and the young potential felon of just a few months prior, suddenly found himself reading Baudelaire and wandering through the catacombs underneath Paris. It was a coming-of-age that Bob Dylan would have killed for.

"I was in heaven—I had a job, I was playing guitar and getting paid for it," he said. "All of a sudden, I went from the depths of despair to one of the greatest times of my life. Looking back, I think I would have told that kid in jail to hang on, everything's gonna be all right."

Meeting Butch and Jimmie (Jimmie years before Butch), and forming the Flatlanders at the 14th Street house in 1971, jump-started Ely's songwriting engine. "Back in the days when the three of us first got together, both Butch and Jimmie were such inspirations to me to start writing songs. I mean, I'd written a few before then, but hearing Jimmie write 'Tonight I Think I'm Gonna Go Downtown' and 'Treat Me Like a Saturday Night' and 'Dallas,'" he told *Lone Star Music* magazine, "those are just magic songs for me. And I can see the pictures that Butch paints, and I feel like they came out of my life. Like when I first heard him do 'Boxcars' . . . that song just burned into me. That's what really made me sit down and say, 'I can do that, too.'"

The hitchhiking, road-warrior years gave him all the fodder he needed, he said in an interview with Christopher Oglesby.

"Some of the best stuff I ever wrote was in Lubbock, when I'd get back from my travels, because there is this empty desolation that I could fill if I picked up my pen and wrote, or picked up a guitar and played. Anybody that ever came from there knows that feeling; that big ol' sky and that lunatic desolation; what the wind does to you, the way it rubs the tree branch against the screen all night long. . . . You get pissed off because it's blowing all the time and you're eating all this dust! You dealt with it in whatever way you could."

* * *

There's still time for Heaven
Though we're already there

"Braver Newer World"
JIMMIE DALE GILMORE

———

Jimmie Dale Gilmore's father played electric guitar in a band with the how-perfect-is-that name of the Swingeroos.

That was not long after VJ Day, and Brian Gilmore's axe—a blue, solid-bodied Fender—might have been one of the first electric guitars in West Texas.

He loved music; he named his son after Jimmie Rodgers, the Singing Brakeman with the high and lonesome blue yodel.

The elder Gilmore was raised in the Primitive Baptist Church, and the shaped-note singing of that congregation co-existed in his musical universe alongside another Holy Trinity—Rodgers, Hank Williams, and Ernest Tubb. He loved early rock 'n' roll, too, unlike many of his adult contemporaries. He took Jimmie Dale and his sister to see Johnny Cash and Elvis Presley at the South Plains Fairgrounds Coliseum in Lubbock, in the spring of 1956, an experience the teenage boy remembered as being "louder than anything else I'd ever heard."

Brian Gilmore wasn't a full-time, professional musician. He and the guys he sat in with played VFW dances and parties and picnics as well as the occasional beer joint. He and his wife, Mary, had a dairy farm outside of Tulia, a tiny spot halfway between Amarillo and Lubbock. "Just a little bitty town," as Jimmie remembered it. Perhaps in his mind's eye he pictures it in black-and-white, like an old Walker Evans photograph.

Though he was born in Amarillo, Jimmie lived on that farm until he was about five, when the family moved to Lubbock so Brian could enroll in dairy industry courses at Texas Tech.

"Music in the house was the radio," Jimmie said. "Around the time I was in second grade, we got a little 45-rpm record player. One of the first records I had was [Gene Autry's version of] 'Rudolph the Red-Nosed Reindeer.' That made a very deep impression on me."

That's the way it's always been for Gilmore—country and rockabilly in one ear, folk music and Christmas carols out of the other. In a deeply ecumenical way, it's all the same to him. All of it is like planets orbiting around the sun of Gilmore's musical imagination, each equally important and valuable in its way.

"I am a folk musician," he said one day. "I am a traditionalist. But the tradition that I was born into was a whole bunch of radio music. And the folk music that I'm a product of is everything from Hank Williams and Elvis and Little Richard to Joan Baez, Chuck Berry, and Brenda Lee."

Or, as he put it another way, "I never fell into any of the categories. . . . I sure didn't toss out my Lefty Frizzell records when I discovered the Beatles."

Gilmore is happy to throw all his influences into the cosmic blender and let them resurface in his music like raisins in a cake. But what knits the synthesis of his repertoire together is his otherworldly, yearning, high-lonesome tenor voice. (When he was four, Brian told the *New York Times*, "He could sing Hank Williams songs all the way through. He'd go out on the haystack with his Aunt Janie. Jimmie would sing and Janie would cry.")

That voice, not the guitar, is his true instrument, and once you've heard Jimmie Dale Gilmore sing, you can't get him out of your head. Like Johnny Cash, Leonard Cohen, or Billie Holiday, he is a unique vocalist who transforms everything he sings.

Described variously as "a wide, quavering voice that sounds like a 78 rpm record with scratches" (the *New York Times*), "a voice with the kind of resonance and feeling that pricks up ears [and] turns heads" (*Texas Monthly*), and "beautifully spare" (*Esquire*), Gilmore's singing voice twangs with a flat, earthbound nasal West Texas accent that still manages to float like a nightingale.

The *Esquire* writer paid Gilmore perhaps the ultimate compliment, writing about a cover tune on Gilmore's 1993 album, *Spinning Around the Sun*: "Maybe Hank Williams sang a better 'I'm So Lonesome I Could Cry.' Maybe not."

Gilmore's voice is the aural equivalent of the Texas Panhandle landscape, the distillation of an austere and desolate beauty so striking and minimal that Georgia O'Keeffe painted the Palo Duro Canyon dawn horizon over and over again, trying to capture its essence.

The first voice that fans of the Flatlanders ever heard on record was Jimmie's, singing what is still perhaps the most potent and poignant image he's ever created: "Have you ever seen Dallas from a DC-9 at night?" Another vocalist might use the line to convey anticipation, but Gilmore (twenty-seven at the time) sings it with the melancholy echo of unredeemed dreams—the lights are only beautiful from a distance.

"I always liked Hank Williams just as much as the Beatles," he says today. "But not more so. None of that stuff is out of my range of influences. But nobody ever realizes it, because my voice is so thoroughly imprinted with that Hank Williams/ Jimmie Rodgers vibe. The automatic assumption is that that's all I can do. But that's never been true, even back in the Flatlanders days."

Ironically, Jimmie gravitated naturally to the acoustic guitar, rather than the electric model favored by his father. As a result, he says, today he can only just get around on the electric guitar.

"I actually met Earl Scruggs backstage one night in Lubbock," Gilmore recalled. "And he was best known as a banjo player, of course, but he gave me some good guitar advice. He told me to get myself a Gibson Country & Western guitar. I wore it out entirely."

It was the era of Bob Dylan and Joan Baez and a thousand folkie-wannabes. It's telling that Gilmore and Butch Hancock both gravitated to the acoustic guitar universe, while Joe Ely made a beeline for the Stratocaster.

Gilmore also played trombone in the school band during his junior high days at W. B. Atkins in Lubbock. That's where, in 1957, he met Butch Hancock. He met Ely later, outside of school. "We discovered each other played music, but we didn't play together," he said. That would come in time.

In the meantime, like everyone else, he was listening to Buddy Holly and Roy Orbison, the two West Texas boys–made–good. And, in one of those odd bits of Lubbock propinquity, in 1964 or '65 he met Larry Holley, Buddy's father. The older man became something of an early mentor to Gilmore and offered to stake him to his first recording session, a five-song demo. To this day, Jimmie doesn't know what happened to the tapes.

Suddenly, Gilmore needed a band to record. He enlisted Ely, guitarists John X. Reed and Jesse Taylor, drummer T. J. McFarland, and a pretty girl with a powerhouse voice named Angela Strehli (Angela's reclusive brother Al would, in time, become a valuable contributor of songs to the Flatlanders and to Gilmore personally).

They called themselves the T. Nickel House Band, after a friend named Tommy Nickel, in whose home they would practice.

"Mr. Holley paid for me to make some demos, so I put a band together. My first band ever," he said. "We played around town some, and then Joe left town and for a while the T. Nickel

House Band was me and John and T. J. and Jesse. I played bass. I wasn't very good, which was one reason the band wasn't very good."

The demo came to nothing, and he became, by his own admission, pretty much a vagabond for the latter half of the sixties.

One of his paths led him to Austin and that city's blooming fusion of country, rock, and folk. Gilmore put together a second band, a trio called the Hub City Movers, to play Austin clubs like the Vulcan Gas Company and the One Knite. "Insane, psychedelic country folk-rock," was how he described their sound. John X. Reed and T. J. McFarland from the T. Nickel House Band joined him in the group.

Gilmore, by several accounts, managed to be present at a near-mythical creation moment in Austin's musical history.

One night in 1970, the Hub City Movers were playing the Cactus Club, a long-vanished venue on the corner of Riverside Drive and Barton Springs Road. The band was on break and the men's room was crowded, so Gilmore, Reed, and a gregarious ex–beer lobbyist named Eddie Wilson went out back to attend to business.

According to lore, Wilson looked up at the building next door, a hulking, empty former National Guard armory, perfect for a hippie concert hall. In one of those "Eureka!" moments that still figures in the city's "Keep Austin Weird" mantra, Wilson said he'd gotten the idea for the city's beloved Armadillo World Headquarters by the time he'd zipped up his pants. The Hub City Movers played the 'Dillo's opening night.

By the time Gilmore spent several months in Austin, he'd already put on some miles, in literal and figurative fact.

He'd already married for the first time, to Jo Carol Pierce, who'd been his high school sweetheart, and had fathered a daughter.

"Jimmie and I moved to California several times," Jo Carol told writer Richard Gehr. "The first time was in 1964, when our daughter Elyse was five weeks old, with $60 and an old Rambler. But we'd always get busted back to Lubbock. We thought it was some kind of Indian curse."

(Pierce went on to a multifaceted career as an actress, songwriter, and playwright; the two remained fast friends, even after the marriage foundered. Today Jo Carol fondly refers to Jimmie's current spouse, Janet, as her "beautiful wife-in-law.")

Like Ely, Gilmore had been influenced by the Beats and their rootless wanderings. Unlike them, he had no amphetamine-fueled rush to get out and *be*. "I didn't have a car," he said. "I felt like what happened was, my whole circle of friends were a support group and I was mentally ill. I slept on people's couches and they fed me. It was sort of like, I was always working on a career, but not really. I was just . . . at loose ends." He worked as a maintenance man in a Lubbock hospital when he moved home from Austin in 1971.

Gilmore was lucky—or perhaps the right word is "blessed"— to have a safety net in Lubbock to catch him.

As noted in a previous chapter, "It was a group of friends that grew and grew, and most of them weren't musicians. There were all these different circles that came together— highly creative people who also felt stultified by Lubbock. It was like huddling together for warmth in such a repressive kind of atmosphere.

"That group was the incubator that made the Flatlanders. We didn't have nightclubs or venues, but we had this circle of friends. The Flatlanders were a laboratory for the ideas we were into. There was an intellectual backdrop in it that was real."

Butch and Joe, he said, fit in in their own way. "Some of us got into peyote when it was still legal. Butch never did do the drug thing. He wasn't as wild as we were. And Joe was from a circle of friends that were wilder than us. That means they were already over the edge—outright criminals, some of them."

Music is what bound the three, and the friendship that developed from music is what keeps them bound forty years later.

"Even now, it's a greater thrill if these guys like my songs than if I had a million seller that they thought was lackluster," Gilmore told the *New York Times*. "There was a time, you know, when we were each other's only audience."

Down in my hometown there is a fortune
They used to call it gold, but now it's love I'm told

"Down in My Hometown"
JIMMIE DALE GILMORE

It was also around this time, the late sixties, that the parallel forces of making music and spiritual seeking began to manifest themselves in Gilmore's life (Jimmie, being Jimmie, would insist that they aren't parallel at all—they're the same thing).

A friend named Max Cheshire gave Gilmore a copy of W. Somerset Maugham's *The Razor's Edge*, the story of a traumatized American searching for transcendent meaning in his life in the years after World War I. The epigraph of the book is from a Buddhist text: "The sharp edge of a razor is difficult to pass over; thus the wise say the path to Salvation is hard."

The book had a huge impact on Gilmore. "My receptors were really wide open. I had mostly read science fiction and comic books up to that point. Max turned my reading in a quality direction. More than any schoolteacher."

From there, it was a short step to the Beats.

"Jack Kerouac was having as much of an effect on us as Elvis was," he said. "Kerouac was an avowed Buddhist. He and Gary

Snyder and Allen Ginsberg. Kerouac wrote a book called *Wake Up*. 'Buddha' means 'the awakened one.' There was a legendary encounter when someone asked him if he was a god, and he said no. He was asked if he was a man, and he said no. Well, then, what are you? And he answered, 'I am awake.'

"His teaching was that love and consciousness are the same thing. It's really in agreement with all religions at the core. But the approach was to wake up, so there you had Kerouac's book.

"When we first got together, Butch and Joe and I were already reading Krishnamurti [Jiddu Krishnamurti, the Indian author, mystic, and philosopher] and other Eastern spiritual writers. He said the whole thing about gurus was fake and you had to find the truth on your own. I disagreed with a lot of his philosophy, but not all of it. I disagree with him in some ways.

"But the point is, we were enmeshed in Oriental philosophy before the Flatlanders. I was already on that train. We were all explorers on a much bigger train than just the music.

"From reading, I decided I needed to learn how to meditate. I had been reading *Vedanta for the Western World* [a collection of essays edited by Christopher Isherwood] and *The Perennial Philosophy*, by Aldous Huxley. I was already looking. I came to the conclusion that I needed a guru."

Jimmie and the other Flatlanders went and saw a visiting mahatma (holy person) one time when the band was in Austin. "All the Flatlanders went to see this mahatma. He was very interesting and amazing and I loved it, but he was crazy. He was *really* crazy."

But another spiritual leader would have a far deeper impact on Gilmore's life: "It was also in that period, late '72, it was on one of those trips to Austin that I first became aware of Maharaji."

(Prem Rawat, also known as Maharaji or Guru Mahara Ji, was born the son of a holy man in India in 1957. As leader of the Divine Light Mission, he became a controversial figure in the West, both derided as a cult leader and esteemed as a "satguru," or True Guru—a spiritual teacher and guide. Today he heads up the Prem Rawat Foundation, a group dedicated to humanitarian work and spreading Rawat's teachings.)

Years later, after the Flatlanders' first album was rediscovered, fans would spin Gilmore's spiritual quest into a sort of cathartic breakdown. "People from a distance always presumed [I found Maharaji] because, oh my god, the band fell apart, so I'll go to India!" said Gilmore with a smile. "But it was never that way."

Perhaps, thought Gilmore, here was the teacher he'd been seeking. "I was initiated into Maharaji's meditation system in New Orleans in 1973." The connection was forged through Maharaji's "applicant ashram," whose members had applied for status as an "official" ashram in that city.

The connection was initiated, but not forged. The wandering continued. He returned to Lubbock, married Debby Fields, aka "Little Deb" (now Debby Savage), and moved out to New Mexico to join Tommy X. Hancock, who had relocated out there with his family band. It was familiar territory from trips Gilmore and the other Flatlanders had made to study Sufi dancing and other disciplines at the Lama Foundation retreat center and spiritual community near Taos.

In 1974, Gilmore and Debby (who was pregnant with his son Colin, who is today a successful singer/songwriter on his own) moved to Denver, where Gilmore entered the world headquarters of Maharaji's Divine Light Mission community.

And there the story might have ended. Gilmore studied meditation, absorbed Maharaji's teachings, and, for a time, swept floors at a synagogue. He retreated from music and, said a 1995 *New York Times* profile, "played very little."

Meanwhile Joe Ely, bless his heart, kept Gilmore's name in front of Texas music fans via his own recorded versions of Jimmie's songs.

All this personal history might be not so much about much were it not for the spirituality that pervades so much of Gilmore's music.

In the title track to his 1993 album *Spinning Around the Sun*, Gilmore marries the East and West Texas in a lyrical skein: "I've seen crimson roses growing through a chain-link fence / I've seen crystal visions, sometimes they don't make sense."

Back in the Flatlanders' first incarnation, Gilmore lyrics like "Tonight I think I'm gonna go downtown / Tonight I think I'm gonna look around / For something I couldn't see / When this world was more real to me" had an ethereal, transcendental cast (the song, it should be noted, was cowritten with John X. Reed). Even his growling, rocking, bluesy "Midnight Train" contains cosmic imagery: "You may sit beside fear and go worse than lonely / Or travel with trust, with love and faith restored / These choices you have / And these choices only . . ."

If Ely's songwriting calling cards are the highways and the outcasts that ride them, and Hancock's are playful wordplay and dusty Panhandle imagery, then Gilmore's trademark is a questing, ineffable journey toward the self.

"I've been a spiritual seeker in need of something to save me from my craziness," he said. "That's the underlying story. Music and spirituality are very connected in my world."

But it was a long quest. Gilmore (in the company of the Flatlanders) made his first album in 1972. It would be sixteen years before he would record another.

* * *

She said if you're from Texas, son
Where's your boots and where's your gun
I smiled and said I've got guns no one can see

"She Never Spoke Spanish to Me"
BUTCH HANCOCK

Butch Hancock first learned to write songs in the key of International Harvester.

He'll tell you so himself: "My dad was in the earthmoving business around Lubbock, doing leveling and terracing for farmers," he said to writer Christopher Oglesby.

"He would have me out there after school, on weekends, all summer, driving tractors. I took a harmonica out there and figured out that the key of G was second gear on that ol' tractor. Somewhat exaggerating the speedup and slowdown, you could play any tune you wanted with the tractor."

As an origin story, it's not exactly up there with Robert Johnson selling his soul to the Devil at the crossroads, but it does speak a lot to Hancock's creative process of internalizing the energy of his surroundings. "My theory is that all of the rhythms in your environment imprint a pattern over everything in your unconscious."

Pretty high-falutin' creative theory from a guy who would one day pen the homespun lines "All the boys down at the pool hall got my number / And some gal up in some hotel's got my shoes."

If Jimmie Dale Gilmore is the voice of the Flatlanders, and Joe Ely is the rhythmic engine, then Butch Hancock is the songwriter's pen. Not that the other two aren't graceful, prolific, and accomplished wordsmiths, but neither of them comes close to Butch's repertoire in terms of sheer volume.

To paraphrase Little Richard, the boy can't help it.

In the course of his absurdly prolific career he has composed songs that range from the not-quite-two-minutes "I Grew to Be a Stranger" to the twenty-seven-minutes-plus "Last Long Silver Dollar."

And then there is this: In early 1990 Hancock launched a six-night stand at the Cactus Café, Austin's beloved acoustic listening room. Over the course of that residency, dubbed *No 2 Alike*, he performed 140 pieces of original material without repeating a song. He figured at the time that the marathon represented about half his repertoire.

"I would say his songs have gotten longer over time," said Joe Ely, who, along with Gilmore, has made a cottage industry out of covering Butch's songs. "But that's impossible.

"There's a category of ones you remember and a category of ones that, every time you hear them, you experience them like they were brand-new.

"It's a feeling that I've been there and gone through the same experience," like the way he internalized "Boxcars" the first time he heard Butch play it.

Ely told *Dirty Linen*, "I'd grown up around the rail yards in Amarillo—all these trains running west and east, and I wondered where they went. Butch's song added a spirituality to it that is haunting and uplifting at the same time."

"Butch's love of wordplay was obvious to me right away," said Jimmie Dale Gilmore, who's known Hancock since junior high. "And he plays so well that he can get away with playing rough, and the contrast of that rough sound with these brilliant . . . *things* is so striking.

"His stuff was so far ahead of anything Nashville was doing—and it still is. But back then [when the Flatlanders went to Nashville in 1972 to record], it was just *out of this world*. They understood that it was great, but they also understood that people wouldn't know what to think if they heard these weird, crazy images on the radio." (Nonetheless, Emmylou Harris scored when she made Butch's loveliest song, "If You Were a Bluebird," the title track of her 1989 album, *Bluebird*. She also covered his playful "West Texas Waltz.")

Though he may have been too unconventional for commercial radio, Hancock wrote the kind of songs, said Michael Ventura, "that could find their way out of a bar and follow you home."

When Gilmore cites Butch's "love of wordplay," that is an assessment of Everest-sized understatement. Rhymes, allusions, populist political fervor, metaphors, shaggy-dog stories, lovers' laments, puns (he is a black-belt-level punster), surreal Dalí-like landscapes, irony, classical and pop references, hard-bitten Dust Bowl snapshots, and the lighthearted byplay of stringing together words for the sheer joy of it—all come flooding out of his pen like water gushing from a Hill Country spring.

He can conjure up an image with a razor's efficiency: "Carmen must have been the Devil's daughter / At least he taught her how to wear her clothes."

Or he can indulge in a couplet corny enough to melt an iPod: "I said close up your windows, go lock up her vaults / And let's go dance like the dickens to the West Texas Waltz."

The requisite horizon-piercing highways, bottles of booze, and broken hearts of country music dot his songs like so many chocolate chips, but he gives the timeworn elements a deft twist that takes an unexpected meander into metaphysical latitudes ("Firewater," he sings, "seeks its own level").

In Butch Hancock's world, every raindrop is eternally suspended between Heaven and the hard Texas earth, and every train is bound for glory. Life and love flicker as elusively as heat lightning out on the western horizon.

Put it another way—if a pickup truck with Lewis Carroll and Will Rogers ran a stop sign in Wichita Falls and sideswiped a '56 Cadillac with Oscar Wilde and Hank Williams inside and they all went into a beer joint to swap insurance information, they might have collaborated on the best of Butch Hancock's repertoire.

Now Split and Slide were tired and sore
And sick and tired of being so poor
If money was rain, they'd been a seven-year drought
Split said, Slide, that's par for the course;
You talk like a dog, I talk like a horse.
And this here's coming straight from the horse's mouth.

"Split and Slide"

BUTCH HANCOCK

———

Butch Hancock—George Hancock is his given name—was born in Lubbock in July of 1945, not long before VJ Day. "I heard the story that my dad walked into the delivery room and said, 'Hi, Butch,' first thing," he said. "Around the house, I remember getting called that. But sometimes I'd hear, 'George Herman, get out of the kitchen!'"

"He did a lot of camping, he was in the Cub Scouts," his older sister Linda recalled in a 1991 interview. "Dad was a land-leveling contractor. He worked all over the Lubbock area, all around the Caprock."

Linda recalled he got his first guitar in Mexico, on a trip there with his Spanish club. "The next thing we knew," she said, "he would have his door closed and be plucking away in his room.

"Either when he was in high school or his first year at Texas Tech, my mom and dad were associated with Amway, and he wrote a song about selling Amway products that was just terrific. That's one of the first little ditties I recall him writing.

"Then he became associated with Jimmie and Joe and all that bunch, and they played around in each other's garages for anybody they could find that would put up with 'em."

Hancock grew up in Lubbock with blue-chip West Texas credentials: he was a tractor driver's boy and an Eagle Scout; a schoolboy athlete who ran track and played basketball, one of those scrappy, sawed-off white kids the Panhandle breeds like so many bolls of cotton.

"He wasn't a typical jock, though," recalled Jimmie Gilmore. "He didn't fit into that macho, ego thing, but he got along with that faction real well. I was amazed when I found out he played guitar, because my image of him was entirely different. [But] there was a solid bedrock friendship there before we ever started playing together."

Butch's assessment of his athletic career is typically self-effacing: "I was good at it, but not really, really good at it. I was never quite playing the same game as everybody else, I think. I always felt like I was on the outside, and I think Jimmie did too."

After graduating from Monterey High, Hancock entered Texas Tech to study architecture, the only formal academic field that even slightly interested him. By chance (or cosmic design) he discovered that principles of architecture lent themselves well to songwriting. "Instead of building a building, you're simply building a song. You put together all these weird, totally unrelated things that make something new, coherent, useful, and hopefully beautiful. In songwriting, there has to be melody, rhythm, and all the basic elements of design."

He has always maintained that if you yearn to do something really well, study something else. "In doing so," he told Oglesby, "you're going to be measuring this new thing against your passion."

Eventually, after several false starts and stops, he left architecture school. "I just realized there always had to be a kitchen door somewhere," he said.

He returned to work for his dad for a time, but music began to exert more of a gravitational force on his imagination. Going back through the journals he's kept for decades, he observed,

"Time after time, the last entry of every day was 'played guitars till three a.m.'"

Though all three of the principals arrived back in Lubbock at the same time by coincidence (Ely from his gypsy rambling, Jimmie from Austin, and Hancock himself from the Bay Area, where he had been studying with an architectural photographer), he made their union sound goddamned near inevitable:

"After I dropped out of architectural school for the umpteenth time, I started playing guitar at some parties. And four or five of us wound up playing together more and more consistently, and before long the Flatlanders were born."

He never lost interest in architecture, or building, or design, however. Nor in the futuristic and intricate ballpoint pen sketches, many of fantastical, organic-looking structures, that filled scores if not hundreds of spiral-bound notebooks.

Ely said wryly, "He's always building a bar or a house or diggin' a hole or something. I remember in Lubbock, he was building a . . . something on the outskirts of town. We never figured out quite what it was. He was always moving dirt around, rearranging it, you know?"

It wasn't that Hancock ever had to choose between music or architecture. Or photography or running an art gallery or driving a tractor or journaling or shooting videos or working as a whitewater river guide or any of the other myriad vocations and avocations he's pursued over the decades. It's just a way for him to understand what Buckminster Fuller called the Generalized Principles, and what Butch describes as the way systems interact and impact one another; transformative patterns that repeat.

"I'm still of the mind that we're all fast thinkers out in West Texas, but we're real slow learners," he says.

CHAPTER 6

Compañeros

The story of the Flatlanders is not just the story of Jimmie, Joe, and Butch, although that is how most folks think of the band. There were three more original performers, for one thing—Steve Wesson, Tony Pearson, and (to a much lesser extent) Sylvester Rice—and they played pivotal roles in the group's origin story, the original demo tape they recorded in Odessa, Texas, and the subsequent foray to Nashville that resulted in their legendary and long-unreleased first album. Hell, Steve gave the Flatlanders their name . . . but more about that later.

Additionally, there are a couple of other individuals who, although they never were part of the band, played fundamental roles in the Flatlanders' lives and careers. Ely's, Hancock's, and Gilmore's career trajectories might have been altered considerably had they never met Tommy X. Hancock or C. B. Stubblefield.

★ ★ ★

*I'm the poser in the group. I just surround myself
with other people who make me look good.*

STEVE WESSON

———

Steve Wesson still has the musical saw he played at 14th Street
and on the Flatlanders' 1972 Nashville session. He ordered it
from the *Whole Earth Catalog*, and it is a thoroughly unremark-
able-looking piece of workmanship. Just looks like a damned
old saw.

"You can play any saw," he explained. "But a musical saw is
tempered a little better and holds notes a little longer." Flexing
the saw blade creates the pitch, and one strikes the saw with a
small mallet to create the note.

That warbling, otherworldly wobble and whistle of sound is,
along with Jimmie Dale Gilmore's equally otherworldly voice,
the signature sound of the early Flatlanders. Today, when Wesson is able, he joins his onetime cohorts onstage, and the addition of his musical saw kicks the modern Flatlanders ensemble
forward and backwards, both at once.

He first heard a saw played, he said, on some of Jimmie
Rodgers's old records, and he himself learned to play by ear,
playing along to those songs.

"Always had a good ear," he said. "As a kid, I picked out melodies on the piano. I couldn't pick out what was right, but I
could pick out what was wrong." Learning music was a process
of elimination.

Wesson today lives on a tree-shaded spread outside of
Salado, a small town about fifty miles north of Austin whose
stock-in-trade is mostly galleries, boutiques, and B&Bs. But
his boyhood landscape was a lot less lush and far less green.

Wesson grew up bouncing between Lubbock and Dimmitt, a small Panhandle farming/ranching community between Lubbock and Amarillo.

He went to Texas Tech and got an undergraduate degree in advertising art, and then an MFA, during which time he was a technician with the art department. Music was an avocation, at least until he met Butch Hancock, who was doing roughly the same thing for the adjacent architecture department.

"I went over to Butch's house on 8th or 10th Street one night, and Jimmie and Joe were there," Wesson recalled. "Or Joe might not have been there, I can't recall for sure. Anyway, we sat around and played those old country songs, and I decided I wanted to do something like that."

"Until Steve started hanging with us, I don't think he really played music," said Ely. "He could jam along [but] he kind of invented his own technique and style."

Wesson fit right in at 14th Street. "We mostly just got to be a big bunch of buddies. It was way beyond just music; the music was almost incidental. It just happened to be what everybody did. I don't know what you'd call us, a bunch of quirky folks. We were all searching for a higher meaning, or even just a meaning."

Wesson's search took him out to New Mexico around 1971, where he stopped off at the Lama Foundation spiritual retreat near Taos. "I was on my way to see a friend in Salt Lake City and I stopped on my way up there. There happened to be a Sufi teacher there teaching Sufi dances and I got in the middle of them. That day changed my life forever."

Wesson took word of the vigorous physical meditation technique back to Lubbock, and soon Joe, Sharon, Jimmie, Tommy Hancock, and whoever all else would periodically pile into Butch's van and take off for the Land of Enchantment to become whirling dervishes themselves.

"That was the first time," said Wesson, "that I'd ever had the experience of feeling real love for strangers that I'd never seen before and would never see again."

Wesson's first time in a recording studio was when the Flatlanders recorded their demo in the winter of 1972 in Odessa, the recordings that led to their contract with Shelby Singleton, Jr.'s Plantation Records. The second time was when he walked into one of Music Row's top-shelf rooms in Nashville. No pressure, right?

At this point—in Nashville, fixing to sign a contract and cut an album—the band still didn't have a name. As a lark, they'd been calling themselves the Supernatural Playboys, in honor of the Lubbock health food store at which they sometimes played, and as a tongue-in-cheek spoof of Bob Wills and every other Western Swing band with "Something Playboys" in their name.

This was the sort of hippie foolishness up with which 1972-era Nashville would not put.

The guys were doing what they'd always done, pulling their chairs in a circle and warming up with some songs from their multitudinous repertoire of vintage blues, country, and folk music.

As Wesson recalled, "Jimmy Martin, who used to be with Bill Monroe, just happened to be up in the booth. He'd dropped by to hear us. He came down and met us all, and he's the one who said, 'It takes a bunch of you flatlanders to come out here and show us how to do real hillbilly music.' And it struck me. I said, 'Flatlanders?! That's it. That's our name.'"

Jimmie Dale Gilmore recalled it slightly differently in a radio interview: "We were getting ready to record, and showing him [Royce Clark, the talent scout who was their Nashville liaison] our songs. We played 'Hello Stranger,' or a really old hillbilly song. When we got finished with it Royce said, 'This is so strange for a bunch of flatlanders to come here and teach Nashville people to play hillbilly music.' Steve Wesson looked up and said, 'That's it!' We all just went, 'Yeah!' First of all, it's literally accurate. And we'd been to Colorado and knew flatlanders were always looked down on."

Either way, thanks to Wesson the band had its name.

The band lazed along after the Nashville interlude, playing gigs in Victoria and Austin, winning a surprise spot at the first Kerrville Folk Festival, waiting for the hit-making machinery to grind into gear. It never happened.

"The record never came out, so Joe went to California, Jimmie went to Denver, and I think Butch went to New Mexico for a while and so did I and Tony Pearson," Wesson said. He moved to Salado, and music was once more a hobby, not a career move. He did, however, join the three principals from time to time on occasional one-off reunion shows.

But then came the Flatlanders' 2002 resurrection, and Wesson found himself back in the studio with his old amigos, saw in hand. He's been featured on all three of the Flatlanders' contemporary studio albums, and on stage with them when his schedule and special circumstances permit.

"Tony and I were there," he said with a grin. "Surreal, yeah! I'm a little rube from Dimmitt, Texas, in New York City on the David Letterman show."

Gigging again with the Flatlanders is like the Christmas present you've forgotten about under the tree. "The whole thing is just a gift for me," he said. "Joe and them have been very good to us.

"I never had enough of an ego to let it talk me into living that [musician's] life. But it's been great, very gratifying. And fun."

* * *

Butch and Jimmie and Joe are professional musicians.
I'm an amateur musician—I love music, but I hate
the business of music.

TONY PEARSON

———

Mandolinist, bass player, and harmony vocalist Tony Pearson would deserve a place in the Flatlanders' saga even if he'd
never done anything but turn them on to a certain house in
the Tech Ghetto.

"My wife at the time took the house on 14th Street and
lived there for a couple of years," the Lubbock native recalled.
"Then my grandmother bought a rent house and she asked if
we wanted to live in that house instead. So we moved to the
rent house.

"Jimmie and everyone had been coming to the 14th Street
house, playing music and laughing and whatever. So I said,
'This house will be available if you want to get it.'"

They did. As soon as Pearson moved out, Joe, Jimmie,
Butch, Sharon, and the rest moved right in, and the festivities
commenced. Pearson was hardly a stranger. He and his wife
were on the outs ("I was playing too much music, mostly"),
so after they split up, he found himself back at his old digs as
often as not, camping out with everyone else.

Pearson and his current wife live in Portland, Oregon, now,
where he is retired from a job with Texas Instruments in Dallas.

But he grew up in Lubbock, and, like Jimmie Dale Gilmore,
he had a relative who was a musician, an uncle with the Shake-
spearean handle of Mark Anthony. But unlike Brian Gilmore,
who twanged his Fender guitar in the honky-tonks, Pearson's
uncle rocked the trombone in big bands led by the likes of Blue
Barron and Les Brown. Jazz and swing were his métier, but

Mark Anthony's wife, like Tony's ex, declared that the social ramble wasn't restful.

"He married a woman who said if he didn't come back home to Ralls, Texas, she was gonna divorce him," Pearson said. "So he put up his horn and became a farmer the rest of his life." (Anyone who's been through Ralls, halfway between Idalou and McAdoo, east of Lubbock, can appreciate that this was indeed true love.)

"But he always had a little band [on the side]," Pearson continued, "and anytime anybody came through, he was the go-to guy for backing people up. He backed up Frank Sinatra, people like that, when they came to Lubbock or Amarillo."

As a consequence, Pearson grew up on a more elevated musical plane than the other Flatlanders. He played cello in orchestra and the lower brass instruments in band in school.

He was not, he said, galvanized by the arrival of rock 'n' roll the way many teens in Lubbock were. "I thought it was kid's stuff," he said. "And of course, it *was* kid's stuff. That was its strength, mainly; mostly rhythm, and such simple little chord structures. I had nothing against it. But I was used to written music."

He began to become interested in folk and country music when he and Jimmie began hanging out and playing in high school—the beginning of a friendship that has lasted fifty years. "That was back in 1962 or so, and folk music was just getting off the ground."

Gilmore's dad had an old mandolin lying around, and both boys began fiddling with it one day. From his cello playing experience, Pearson found the fingerings immediately familiar. Jimmie decided to stick to the guitar.

Pearson also met Butch Hancock at Tech; Butch was studying architecture and Tony was librarian for the architecture slides. Next door was the art department, where Steve Wesson worked.

"Steve might have come up with the name 'Supernatural Foods,' said Pearson of the health food store that he and a woman named Laura Hunt opened. Everyone hung out and practiced music in the back, and, as noted previously, for a time the Flatlanders jokingly called themselves the Supernatural Playboys. "We played a lot more music than we sold health food," Pearson said without evident regret.

Like the rest of the nucleus of curious souls who congregated around 14th Street, Pearson explored the literature of the Beats, Eastern spirituality, and whatever other tangent someone was excited about. "Usually," he said, "if anyone in Lubbock had any brains at all, they were already questioning the crap they'd been told all those years. So it just really rang true—'Gosh, Buddhism makes a lot of sense!'"

The Flatlanders' forays to Odessa and Nashville were fun, quixotic adventures from Pearson's perspective. And a bit of a challenge, as when he was drafted to play bass on the Odessa sessions.

"Jimmie had borrowed a string bass from a guy in Slaton" to take to the session, said Pearson. "Since I'd played cello, I said, 'Let me try it.' And I was *terrible*! I'd never done it before. So anyway, I was playing bass, then Joe played for a little bit on some of the songs. It's not great bass playing, at all." (The liner notes for the 2012 *Odessa Tapes* album also cite Syl Rice as playing bass "on some songs." Pearson said he doesn't recall that being the case.)

To Pearson, looking back with forty years' hindsight, the demo recordings the band made in Odessa remain the essential distillation of what the Flatlanders were all about.

"That purity is just not in any of the other recordings," he asserted. "To me, the original Odessa one is the real deal. That's what we sounded like. Naïveté, at least to me, is the essential component of all that was Flatlander. If we'd known what we were doing, it wouldn't have occurred."

Citing the eternal Lubbock mantra, Pearson said of the Nashville sojourn, "We didn't have anything better to do." But when the record fell flat, his perspective didn't change: "I'm an amateur musician—I love music, but I hate the business of music." Pearson had his degree in the classics—Latin and Greek. A music business career was never on his dance card.

Still, he's proud of having played on all of the band's recordings, both old and new, and prouder still of the enduring friendships he's carried through the years. "Every time we get together, it's like family."

* * *

He was "West Texas friendly." . . . A dear sweetheart.

BUTCH HANCOCK
on Sylvester Rice

Less is known about Sylvester Rice than the other members of the Flatlanders, in part because he's not around to speak for himself; he died in October of 2003. But his story is important because of the role he played as a facilitator in getting the band to Odessa to record its demo tape, and thence to Nashville. Additionally, he was the custodian of what came to be known as "the Odessa Tapes," although "custodian" may be too grandiose a word; the tapes sat at the back of a dark, cool shelf in his closet in Lubbock for three decades or so, forgotten by almost everyone. Still.

Ironically, a Los Angeles sound engineer examining the tapes for Joe Ely told him that Rice's closet was the ideal preservation environment.

Rice played bass on the Flatlanders' Nashville sessions, and he might have played with them occasionally around Lubbock as well, but he was never an intimate part of the group's far-flung, yet closely knit, extended group. Nor was he a regular member of the 14th Street crowd. Tony Pearson recalls him showing up "a couple of times."

For one thing, he was older than most of that crew, by ten or fifteen years. He ran with a different crowd, mainly the established bandleaders and local deejays in Lubbock, and he hung around Don Caldwell's fledgling recording studio. And he held down a series of "real" day jobs in real estate and the title business.

"He was way more conventional than us," said Steve Wesson.

"He was tall and had curly red hair—a unique-looking character," said Lloyd Maines, who knew Rice through his own steel guitar session work at Caldwell's. "He was never a full-time professional player, but he was a really smart guy. He'd hang out at Caldwell's and drink coffee. A couple of nights a week, he'd play bass for Wilburn Roach at the Western-Aire Lounge."

Perhaps through that connection, or perhaps another, Rice got to know Brian Gilmore, Jimmie's dad, he of the blue Fender electric guitar.

"Syl knew Brian, and Brian said, 'You've got to come hear my son sing,'" Maines said. He also became friends with Nubby Mattison, the father-in-law of Jimmie's sister.

"It's interesting," noted Butch Hancock. "As you grow up in Lubbock, you see almost everybody and later you find out someone is someone's cousin or something. Those circles keep coming around."

Rice must have taken the elder Gilmore's advice and checked out Jimmie Dale and his buddies and urged his deejay friends to do the same.

"I met Syl through the radio station guys who came out to see my band," said Joe Ely. "We'd sometimes play the bar above the Koko Inn, and these radio guys, Country Lou D and Sylvester, would come out."

"Country Lou D" was Louis Driver, a disc jockey at KDAV,

the big local country station that has been cited as one of the first in the nation (if not the first) to boast an all-country format. He was "Country" Lou D to distinguish him from another deejay, Lew Dee, over at the pop station KSEL.

In those days, lower-echelon touring acts sometimes bunked at the homes of local deejays. "Lou D brought Willie Nelson to the Town Pump to hear us play one night," Ely said of one Flatlanders gig. "We all knew Willie from his songs and he used to come to the Cotton Club when he played with Ray Price. He was very Nashville-looking at the time." The Flatlanders would later record Willie's "One Day at a Time" during their Nashville tenure.

A disc jockey connection was important, even if you didn't have a record to flog. "Back in those days," continued Ely, "the only way you'd get recorded was via a radio station," which, absent a good local recording studio, was the only place with the appropriate technology. At that time, according to Lloyd Maines, Caldwell's was not yet in that league; it was a good place for local farmers to come in and record gospel music.

Anyway, Rice liked what he heard well enough to put his money where his mouth was. "Syl and Lou D decided they were gonna be our managers, and it just happened that he played bass, too," said Wesson.

"That whole scene of Country Lou D and Syl was what instigated our going to Odessa to record," said Ely. "Syl paid for the session."

(Jimmie Dale Gilmore slightly disputes that last point: "Lou D and Syl put together the money to take us over to Odessa to do the tape. Between them, that's where the money came from. I guarantee it wasn't much, not much more than a couple of hundred dollars.")

Whatever the case, Rice was sold on the Flatlanders, although he knew it was a crapshoot. "When he started helping the guys, they were totally wet behind the ears," said Maines. "Syl told me, 'I knew it was risky money, 'cause they were fly-by-night vagabond hippies.'"

Rice helped make the connection that put the Flatlanders on the road to Music City. "Nubby Mattison had introduced us to Syl Rice," said Jimmie Dale in the liner notes to *The Odessa Tapes*. "Syl introduced us to his radio friends, including Lou Driver. Syl and Lou became our 'managers.' Lou asked Joe and I over to his house when record producer Royce Clark was in town, and had us play a couple of songs for him. He said he wanted to make a record with us but would need a demo to show his boss [Shelby Singleton] in Nashville. That was the instigation of the Odessa trip."

The demo got them signed to Singleton's Plantation label. The guys had, in large part, Sylvester Rice to thank.

Rice, Lou D, and Nubby Mattison, according to Maines, put up the money for the Flatlanders to go to Nashville.

Rice wound up playing bass on the Nashville sessions, the only time he recorded with the band. "We went downtown to Roy Acuff's store and rented a bass for him," said Wesson.

Though he fell out of their orbit not long thereafter, he became the guardian of a big chunk of the Flatlanders' legacy. Because he paid for them (or, according to Jimmie, partially paid for them), the master tapes from the Odessa demo sessions reverted to him and sat untouched on top of that closet shelf, waiting for their turn in the spotlight.

At last, ailing with the lung cancer that eventually claimed him, he offered to sell the tapes to the guys to defray part of his medical expenses. Thanks to Rice's stewardship, the Odessa Tapes would finally see the light of day.

"He was 'West Texas friendly,' no matter what," Butch Hancock recalled fondly. "Real good-natured and smart. A dear sweetheart."

* * *

Ladies and gentlemen, I'm a cook.

C. B. STUBBLEFIELD

———

Today you can buy Stubb's Bar-B-Q Sauce from coast to coast. But in the beginning, there was only C. B. Stubblefield, "Stubb" to family and friends, of whom there were a multitude.

Stubb charmed the working-class black folks and broke-ass musicians who came into his tiny restaurant on East Broadway Street in Lubbock, just as easily as he charmed Johnny Cash and David Letterman and other celebs when he got famous, thanks to those same broke-ass musicians. He didn't care about a person's station in life—he just wanted, in his own words, "to feed the world." And even rich and famous folks had to eat.

Christopher B. Stubblefield was born in 1931 in the small East Texas farming town of Navasota, the same town that gave rise to the great country bluesman Mance Lipscomb. His daddy, a preacher, moved the family to Lubbock in the 1930s.

Stubb got his start cooking thanks to Uncle Sam. He was part of the all-black Ninety-Sixth Field Artillery unit during the Korean War, in which capacity he was twice wounded. As a mess sergeant, he also oversaw food prep for thousands of GIs.

He mustered out of the service in 1967 and returned to Lubbock, where his eye fell on a tiny dilapidated building at 108 East Broadway—literally across the tracks in East Lubbock, historically the black part of town. He painted it white with red trim, painted "Legendary Bar-B-Q" on the side, plugged in a jukebox stuffed with vintage blues and R&B, and started smoking meat. He hung up a big sign on the inside: "There Will Be No Bad Talk or Loud Talk In This Place."

He was almost too large for his own joint. Stubb was six and a half feet tall, with hands the size of small hams. The original building only held seventy-five people, and it never expanded much beyond that. Today, on East Broadway, there is a memorial to him and his barbecue shack consisting of the slab of the original building and a big, slightly-larger-than-life bronze statue by Terry Allen portraying Stubb with a rack of ribs. Looking at the concrete footprint of the building today, one comes away marveling at how much great music and great food came out of such a tiny space.

Lubbock musicians and Stubb came together thanks in large part to guitarist Jesse Taylor. He was back in Lubbock from California for a time, and, broke-ass musician that he was, he was renting a cheap place out on East Broadway. He had no car, so anytime he wanted to hang with amigos like Joe or Jimmie, he would walk or hitchhike. He passed by the little barbecue shack with the jukebox blaring the blues through the open door many times, and he could never quite summon up the nerve to go inside. But he wanted to, real bad.

"One day," he recounted in Oglesby's *Fire in the Water, Earth in the Air*, "I was hitchhiking and this big Cadillac pulled up. I look into the car and it was Stubb.

"He stops his car in front of Stubb's and said, 'This is where I'm going.' I said to Stubb, 'I've walked by this place so many times and never have been in. Do you go in here very much?'

"Stubb said, 'Sir, I own the place!'

"I said, 'Really? I've always wanted to go in there.'

"Then Stubb said to me, his exact words, 'I'll tell you what. I've got a barbecue sandwich and a cold beer that's got your name on it in there.'"

Jesse started bringing his white musician friends around, and Stubb got in the habit of cooking a big turkey dinner on Sundays and feeding the skinny guitar players and songwriters.

Thus evolved a regular Sunday night jam session, and a kind of fraternity evolved out of smoke, music, food, camaraderie, and a sort of bemused disdain for what all the straight folks in the other Lubbock across the railroad tracks were up to. Poor bastards over there, they never knew what they missed.

"Lubbock reminds me of a huge monster that fell out of the sky," Stubb would tell writer Richard Gehr with a chuckle. "Every once in awhile it moves, but they don't know who to call in to kill the damn thing."

He would, when the spirit moved him, occasionally take off his apron, crowd onto the tiny stage with whoever was playing, and launch into either "Summertime" or "Stormy Monday."

Stubb's became a clubhouse for Lubbock musicians, a place kindred in spirit if not in sensibility to the 14th Street house.

"To me, he was like the father I lost when I was a kid," remembered Ely.

Musicians in other cities heard about the food and the music and began to drop in when the road took them through Lubbock. A young Stevie Ray Vaughan stopped in to peruse the jukebox and returned to play several times. George Thorogood, Muddy Waters, and Linda Ronstadt dropped by (Ms. Ronstadt ordered a Perrier with her barbecue, to the mystification of Stubb and the regulars). He took it all in stride.

One night, hit-making songwriter Tom T. Hall and Joe Ely got up a pool game in the back room. Sharon, Joe's sweetie, wanted the boys to quit playing pool and come out and join her and her amigas. Joe declined, so, when no one was looking, Sharon pocketed the cue ball, assuming that would end the game.

It did not. Ely went to the kitchen, came out with a white onion, and chalked up his stick. Cue ball be damned.

Ely won the game, but Hall got a great song out of it: "The Great East Broadway Onion Championship of 1978," which he recorded on his *Places I've Done Time* album.

Stubb had to close his joint in 1985 due to troubles with what he often called "the RIS," one of his many malapropisms (if he talked about being inaugurated into, say, the Barbecue Hall of Fame, he might speak of his forthcoming "inoculation").

"I got run out of Lubbock 'cause I was broke, busted and disgusted," he told *Texas Monthly*. "You can't fight the IRS with barbecue and sauce."

Like so many of his music friends, he relocated to Austin and cooked for a time for Clifford Antone at Clifford's famous blues club before opening his own place.

In 1991, Ely played *Late Night with David Letterman* and took with him several homemade bottles of Stubb's Bar-B-Q Sauce for the host and crew. Intrigued, Letterman invited Stubb himself onto the show. He asked Stubb how he got interested in cooking. "I was born hungry," he replied. His secret ingredient? "Love and happiness."

Oh, yeah, that sauce. Sharon and Joe lobbied Stubb to bottle his sauce as a way to bring in some extra money. He cooked up a batch in their kitchen, bottled it in recycled jelly jars and whiskey bottles, and slapped a homemade label on it.

Sharon and her friend, songwriter Kimmie Rhodes, dolled themselves up in boots and cowboy hats and drove around handing out samples. Flash forward—in 2012 Stubb's Legendary Bar-B-Q company did about $20 million worth of business. Stubb's grandsons, Rocky and Reggie, are still active in the company.

Stubb did not live to see his mug on every grocery store shelf in America. Illness took him in 1995, but not before he was deep into planning a new club and restaurant.

The new Stubb's Bar-B-Q, on the corner of 8th Street and Red River in downtown Austin, opened in a historic stone building that once housed the One Knite club, where the Flatlanders used to play.

One devoutly wishes Stubb could have been around to see the first African American president eat a plate of ribs and brisket at his joint, as President Obama did during a stop in Austin in May 2013.

Stubb's remains one of the most popular food and music venues in the city, and Stubb's legacy lives on through it.

"Barbecue," he liked to say, "is eternal. It's like the Mississippi River; it's big and it's simple and it takes its own sweet time."

* * *

I remember playing at dances and barn dances where you would play until one or two in the morning and then someone would give you money to play another hour, and then another hour, and you might be there until five or six. People virtually danced all night. They worked hard and they played hard.

TOMMY X. HANCOCK,
to *Texas Monthly*

Tommy X. Hancock is, in many ways, the godfather of the Flatlanders, but to define him in only that way would be to diminish him. Author Christopher Oglesby calls him "perhaps the most influential personality in the history of Lubbock music."

As a musician, he led a band, the Roadside Playboys, that took their Western Swing cues from Bob Wills and Milton Brown and, along with Hoyle Nix, the Miller Brothers, and Billy Briggs and the XIT Boys, were one of the dominant dance bands in West Texas for much of the 1950s and early '60s.

As a clubowner, he ran the second incarnation of the Cotton Club from the early 1960s until 1980. Capable of holding 1,600 drinkers and dancers, and located out past the lights of town on the Slaton Highway, the Cotton Club was said to be the biggest venue between L.A. and Dallas. Bands would play, as the saying went, "from nine till fistfight."

The biggest names in country and R&B were on the marquee (in the latter case, some of the shows were integrated, a rare thing in that time and place). Tommy didn't found the Cotton Club, but it flourished under his management.

"The thing I was good at was putting a good band together and throwing a good party," he confided.

His wife, Charlene, who when she met Tommy was the prettiest girl singer in West Texas, recalled for *Texas Monthly*, "Tommy did the booking, his dad ran the front, and his mom ran the concession, which was soft drinks." The bootleggers hanging around out in the parking lot provided what bootleggers invariably provide.

"Under Hancock's direction the club attracted an odd mixture of people: some were of Hancock's generation . . . others were a younger group of musicians," wrote Joe Carr and Alan Munde in their history of West Texas music, *Prairie Nights to Neon Lights*. "This unusual mix of redneck and hippie . . . provided musicians a unique test audience on which to try their music . . . the basis of the 'Lubbock Sound.'"

As a mentor, he influenced three generations of Lubbock musicians, including his own children.

The Crickets' Sonny Curtis said Hancock was "a strong influence on Buddy Holly and us all."

"Tommy gave Buddy some of his first gigs," recalled Jimmie Dale Gilmore. And he added, "Tommy is an important part of the Flatlanders, and that gets overlooked."

And he did it all with a flair and a left-of-center outlook that puts the word "maverick" to shame. Hancock, of all his West Texas dance band contemporaries, is almost certainly the only one to journey to San Francisco, drop acid, and later write a book called *Zen and the Art of the Texas Two-Step*. "As I get older," he says. "I find that life gets weirder."

Tommy Hancock was born in Lubbock just in time for the Depression, in the spring of 1929. He played the violin in the junior high orchestra but didn't have much experience with country music until he joined the service. All of his fellow GIs, upon hearing he was a Texan, assumed he came out of the womb playing "San Antonio Rose," but all he knew was classical music. He picked up the basics during his hitch, via records and his fellow soldiers. When he got out, he wasn't certain what he wanted to do. But he found out pretty quick.

"I took the line of least resistance," he recounted in *Lubbock Lights*. "I got a job playing in a little late-night club from midnight till four in the morning. I got drunk and made five dollars and thought, 'This is my career! I've found my place in life.' I was eighteen."

Danceland, the name of the club, was the proverbial place your mother warned you against. The clientele was rough and their recreational stimulants did nothing to mellow their dispositions.

"The drugs of choice when I was a young man were bourbon and Benzedrine," he continued. "You could put the bourbon in your boot and the Benzedrine in your pocket. That created a certain atmosphere that in later years came to be seen as pretty barbaric."

On the other hand, it made for an easy gig, in a way.

"Drunk cowboys are a blast to play for," he said many years later. "They tend to fight, but they also tend to dance, and that's what I was there for."

"Tommy would have the most popular country-and-western band in town, and he usually ran whatever was the most popular nightclub," said Gilmore.

Hancock used to joke that the Roadside Playboys toured until they ate so many fried-egg sandwiches on the road that they got too big for their uniforms. The nightclub business beckoned.

But the truth was, the Cotton Club was taking up more and more of his time. Between the bootleggers, the drunk cowboys, and the competition ("If a club didn't have any business, the owner would burn it. If it did have business, his competitors would burn it," he told Oglesby), that vocation was getting stale as well.

Then a trip west changed his life. It was 1968 and he'd heard about a party, of a sort, going on out in California. Well, parties were what got Tommy's motor running.

"A buddy and I went out to San Francisco and took acid and had such a good time," he said. "And when we got back, he introduced me to Jimmie Gilmore.

"My whole thing with taking acid was, I want to know God. If there's a God, I want to know him. And Jimmie was the first intelligent person I'd ever run into that was searching for God."

Jimmie, Joe ("Joey" to Tommy), and Butch were making music that was intriguing and, yes, intelligent, but way too genteel for the types of joints Hancock played and booked.

"My band had a drummer and a sound system, and the Flatlanders were just an acoustic group. But it was fun, and it was new music for me."

They would sit in with him at the Cotton Club every once in a while, and his growing interest in Eastern spiritualism led him to accompany them to the Lama Foundation in New Mexico occasionally. An all-around friendship developed.

As far as Tommy was concerned, the Flatlanders were born in the living room of the big house he and Charlene and the kids kept on Lubbock's west side.

"Getting together and playing with these guys was a new bag for me," he remembered. "They were just a group of guys that played music for fun. I'd never played music for fun. I'd been a professional all my life."

But Hancock could see the potential swirling through the trio even in their raw, almost defiantly uncommercial state.

"Joey had a charisma, Jimmie had intelligence, and Butch had so much talent. But I've never guessed very correctly about commercial music," he said with a rueful chuckle. "I was in it for fifty-six years, but I don't know what the fuck's gonna sell."

When the guys went to Nashville to record, they wanted somebody with some solid professional experience along to help ground them. Hancock got the call.

"I didn't want to go. But Jimmie called me and really wanted me to come up. So I went on up there, and I'm glad I did." But, he added, "Nashville looked like an easy place to get put in jail."

A growing affinity for alternative lifestyles and Eastern religion led Hancock and Charlene to pack up the family and leave Lubbock, first for New Mexico and then for Colorado, to live in an isolated communal environment. The kids, including three beautiful daughters named Conni, Holli, and Traci Lamar and a son named Joaquin, lacked the shopping malls and cable TV of their peers, so they took naturally to music.

There was an unconventional love of life, a spiritual emphasis, and a thirst for music and family kinship among the Hancock clan that's hard to explain on paper. But if you want to get a sense of the fun and adventure Tommy and the Supernatural Family Band (as he named the ensemble he and his kids put together) brought to the day-to-day, look no further than the documentary film *Lubbock Lights*, which features home movie footage of the Hancocks playing and dancing the Bunny Hop on the ramparts of Machu Picchu. Now that's a family vacation.

In the early 1980s, the Supernatural Family Band moved to Austin, like so many of their Lubbock peers, and released a slew of excellent independent albums. They held down a long-time residency at a beer joint on North Lamar near the Austin State School for intellectually disabled youngsters. Monitors would bring the kids to see the Hancocks, and they would sway, grin, and generally have a ball. Everyone danced like the dickens.

Even after Tommy quit fronting the group, Charlene and Traci and Conni continued to perform as the Texana Dames.

Tommy Hancock still lives in Austin, in an apartment with a view of Lady Bird Lake. He goes dancing three or four nights a week at the Broken Spoke or the Continental Club. He doesn't miss Lubbock too much, although he loves the music he made there.

"I was an economic prisoner there," he said. "I made an easy living, had a big family and a big club. Lubbock's always been good to me."

And he allowed how the town has taken a turn for the better since the Cotton Club heyday. Grinning, he added, "Lubbock's improved—it's got trees and beer now."

PART THREE   *The Music*

You sure look fine tonight
In the beer-sign light

"Honky-Tonk Masquerade"
JOE ELY

CHAPTER 7

Joe used to say that none of us had a thimbleful of ambition.
But between the three of us, we had a towering lack of ambition.

JIMMIE DALE GILMORE

Genesis

The thing that is startling to realize is that, for all the gravitas
the Flatlanders and their music acquired over the years, their
tenure as an actual, functioning, gig-playing band was startlingly brief. From the time they coalesced around the living
room of the 14th Street house until they went their separate
ways in the wake of their Nashville recording session was only
a year, maybe less.

The fact that they even got together is a study in serendipity. In the spring of 1971, Joe Ely had been knocking around
in Europe; Jimmie Dale Gilmore had made a foray to Austin
with his band, the Hub City Movers; and Butch had been
studying architecture and photography in San Francisco. They
just happened to all show up back in Lubbock more or less
simultaneously.

"I was in touch with both of them," Jimmie told *No Depression* magazine. "And at one point I said to Joe, 'You know, I've
got this friend who writes some really good songs. You gotta

hear him.' So we got together and we stayed up all night playing together and laughing. And that was the beginning of the
Flatlanders."

The core of the group was, of course, Butch, Jimmie, and
Joe, along with Tony Pearson and Steve Wesson and, to a
much lesser extent, Sylvester Rice. Others drifted in and out
of the loosely knit group for short periods, maybe just a handful of times. There was guitarist John X. Reed and the reclusive
songwriter Al Strehli, from whom Jimmie plucked some lovely
songs, including "I Know You" and "Keeper of the Mountain."
There was also a drummer named Tom Jones, an artist named
Jim Eppler, and accordionist Ponty Bone, who would go on
to join the Joe Ely Band. It was Bone who would describe the
Flatlanders' tiny but select group of followers with a wonderful phrase: "small circles of good taste."

Syl Rice, Country Lou D, and Royce Clark might have been
eyeing the group in terms of record deals and radio play, but
there wasn't much thought given among the principals to
building commercial momentum, or any sort of a music career
in the sense that the public tends to think of it.

"We weren't perceiving it through the eyes of someone trying to get into the music business," said Jimmie, laughing at
the very thought.

"The band was never created as a commercial entity, even
though Joe and I were already set on professional [music] careers," he continued. "That band came out of a circle of friends
that had some musicians in it that liked playing together. We
were beatniks!"

Speaking in 2013, he said, "In some people's eyes, it's sort
of miraculous, the whole deal that we're not only a functioning
unit, but that we're still friends. But it's pretty natural, because
the whole band worked that way from the beginning. The Flatlanders came about because we liked each other so much to

begin with. Going off to Nashville and making the record was just a tangent."

One struggles, in looking at their story then and talking to them now, to find any hint of discord or rancor or ego-driven one-upmanship among the trio.

Journalist Richard Skanse gave it a good shot, though, in a cover story for *Texas Music* magazine in 2000:

> . . . 30 years of friendship and not a bump in the road? It's just too good. Out with the skeletons.
>
> "Well," offers Hancock, "there was that nasty credit card scandal of Jimmie's . . ."
>
> "Oh, and that Eskimo girl," Ely adds cryptically.
>
> "And Joe stealing a steamroller—when I got blamed for that," continues Hancock, "there was some friction there."
>
> "We were in prison for a couple of years in Costa Rica," offers Ely. "We were in the same cell, but we didn't talk to each other for weeks."
>
> "That," says Gilmore, "was Butch's fault."

The camaraderie ran deeper than just intersecting musical tastes or similar temperaments or happy geographical proximity. They are bound by a shared search, a yearning to, as the Hindu teacher Ram Dass and a latter-day Flatlanders song say, be here now.

"The three of us have always had a desire to understand everything we can understand," said Joe Ely to the *Statesman*. "And to be very awake and conscious of everything that's going on. That's really all you can do in this universe. You can't be certain of anything. But you can be present."

That deliberate choice—to be awake and conscious and all on the same wavelength—gave the guys a level of creative intimacy that was almost subatomic. Joe might wake up and jot down a song that he had dreamed the night before . . . but in his dream, Butch had written the song and Jimmie was singing it.

It came out in their performances, too.

"Their voices sound great individually, but they also blend," said Lloyd Maines, who has played with and/or produced all three men individually and together. "They sound so different when they're singing by themselves, but when they do harmonies it's almost like they're brothers."

The Flatlanders played informally pretty much every night—hundreds of shows for friends, Ely recalled. But their paying gigs were sporadic and their crowds sparse.

"There'd never be more than ten people whenever we'd play somewhere," said Ely, exaggerating for effect. "But we'd meet other musicians."

Memories can be hazy things, and the Flatlanders shows that folks *can* recall seem almost maddeningly random in retrospect. They played at Tony's and Laura's Supernatural Health Food Store, a place called the Attic in the basement of an ice cream shop, and such coffeehouses as Tech's microscopic bohemian population could support, including a place called Aunt Maudie's Fun House. Debby Savage (aka "Little Deb") said they performed at "maybe the Elks Lodge." Tommy Hancock recalled them playing at the Unitarian Church and one time, he thinks, a state school for, as he put it, "retarded children." One picture in the booklet included with *The Odessa Tapes* CD shows them playing on the commons at Texas Tech.

Their favorite venue, according to Hancock, was a place called the Town Pump.

"It was in a little old strip mall on 4th St.," he said to *No Depression* magazine. "It was sort of a seedy place—gambling, and they say a prostitution ring ran out of there. But it turns out the only trouble we ever ran across down there was from the tenants next door. It was one of those success groups—motivational training, you know. One of them stabbed somebody in the alley one time. I guess they got motivated."

"Syl Rice told me, 'You've got to come hear these guys, they're real unusual, totally off the cuff,'" said Maines. "So, Syl took me to the Town Pump [to see them]. I knew there was something there, but it sort of took me aback. They appeared a little disorganized, and the songs didn't really have arrangements. At the time, I was used to playing in a rehearsed, arranged situation, but I thought it was great."

But what the Flatlanders lacked in big-time shows and professional polish, they more than made up in repertoire.

Ely's background, and natural inclination, were rock 'n' roll. Gilmore was grounded in classic country and Western Swing, and Hancock came out of the wordy, Dylanesque folk music universe. When they came together, each brought something to the table that the other two had largely not experienced.

"Between us, we had hundreds of songs that we knew, and we'd sit up all night and play them," said Ely, speaking at his home in 2012. "It was a vast repertoire of songs. The musicians in Lubbock were from all different worlds. There were the rock guys and the folk guys and I kind of went in between them. I went to Europe for a year, then came back and got with the Flatlanders and I had a whole other repertoire than Jimmie or Butch, and I found their repertoires fascinating."

He searched around on his computer and came up with a scanned image of a couple of Flatlanders set lists to illustrate his point:

Here's Daddy Dave Dudley's truck-driving anthem, "Six Days on the Road," and Hank's "Honky-Tonkin'" and Willie Nelson's "Bloody Mary Morning." Over yonder is the Cajun waltz "Jole Blon," an untitled schottische, Dylan's "One Too Many Mornings," and Flatt and Scruggs's "Salty Dog Blues" and

Buddy's "Peggy Sue." Mix that stuff up with the Lloyd Price/ Elvis hit "Lawdy Miss Clawdy," Blind Lemon Jefferson's "Black Snake Moan," and Townes Van Zandt's "Waitin' Around to Die."

Throw in some originals (mostly by Butch), and you have a pretty good idea of the Flatlanders' home range. "Vast," as Ely says.

With Jimmie singing most of the lead vocals (though not all; their demo and Nashville album tracks give a false impression), Ely's rudimentary learn-while-you-earn Dobro playing, Steve Wesson's ethereal, oscillating musical saw, and Tony Pearson's jaunty mandolin licks, they sounded like nothing going on in the commercial country or pop music worlds in 1971. If they are to be placed in context at all, it would be more fitting to rank them with contemporary Americana groups like the Lumineers or the Civil Wars.

* * *

I never thought that I would ever wonder why
I ever said goodbye
I had my hopes up high

"Hopes Up High"
JOE ELY

———

One night, right before Christmas in 1971, someone—almost certainly Country Lou D—hooked the Flatlanders up with an out-of-town visitor named Royce Clark.

Clark was a Lubbock native, but he had relocated to Nashville, where he was an independent producer for Shelby Singleton, Jr.

Singleton had had a smash hit in 1968 with Jeannie C. Riley's "Harper Valley P.T.A.," and he had his own record label, Plantation, but he was perhaps better known for having purchased the Sun Records label in 1969 from founder Sam Phillips.

Sun, in its glory days, was the home of Elvis, Johnny Cash, Carl Perkins, Jerry Lee Lewis, Roy Orbison, Charlie Rich, Harold Jenkins (better known as Conway Twitty), and Rufus Thomas. Singleton mostly contented himself with licensing material from Sun's master catalog for use in film and television soundtracks, rereleasing material by its early artists, and creating a market for merchandise and apparel featuring Sun's famous crowing-rooster yellow logo. Plantation was one of several labels under the corporate shelter of Sun Entertainment Corporation.

Royce Clark was perhaps not the handsomest man (Lloyd Maines observed, uncharitably, that "you could dip his face in batter and make gorilla cookies"), but he was a lucky one. A sometimes-songwriter, one of his tunes wound up on the B-side of "Harper Valley P.T.A." A biting, funny, *Peyton Place*–like look at small-town hypocrisy by songwriter Tom T. Hall, the song reached Number One on both the pop and country charts and won a Grammy for Best Female Country Vocal Performance. (In another one of those little bits of West Texas propinquity that is woven through the Flatlanders' story, Riley was born Jeanne Carolyn Stephenson in Anson, Texas, about 150 miles southeast of Lubbock.) Every time "Harper Valley P.T.A." spun, Clark got a piece of the action.

"Country Lou D was a good guy," said Jimmie Dale Gilmore, "but . . . a real used-car salesman type. He would have a band that would play at the armory, and all the KDAV fans would come. It was a horrible band and he couldn't sing, but nobody knew the difference. Syl [Rice] played with him. The musicians liked him because he could get gigs. And he loved us."

(Over the years, in writing about Ely, Gilmore, and Hancock, different writers have rendered Louis Driver's name as "Country Lew Dee," "Lew D," and other variations. "Louis Driver" is listed as the writer of the song "Rose from the Mountain," on the Charly and Rounder releases of the Flatlanders'

Nashville sessions, so I have chosen to go with "Country Lou D" in referencing him. Moreover, no one seems to be quite certain of Driver's whereabouts or even if he is still alive. My inquiries and searches as to Driver's current location or date of death have been inconclusive.)

"Joe and I went over to Lou's house, where Royce was staying," Gilmore continued. "We played about three songs for him, and one of them was 'Dallas.' He said, 'This is great, but I have to have something recorded before I show Shelby.' So Lou and Syl put it together to take us over to Odessa to do the [demo] tape."

Odessa was the closest place where they felt they could get a good enough representation of the Flatlanders' left-of-center sound to sell to a Music City producer. Don Caldwell's studio in Lubbock was just getting organized. "It was mainly a music store," said Maines. "There was a little two-track recorder in the back with egg cartons on the wall."

Norman Petty's studio in Clovis, New Mexico, where Buddy Holly had recorded many of his hits, was out of the picture, price-wise. The big commercial rooms, like Dallas's Sumet-Bernet Studio, were similarly out of the question. Odessa it was.

★ ★ ★

The windshield and the radio play sadly through the night
A crazy blazin' fallin' star just passed me on the right
The taillights down the highway fade low and out of sight
And that farmer's dog can only bark, but this cold north wind
can bite

"You've Never Seen Me Cry"
BUTCH HANCOCK

———

Butch was, is, and always will be a compulsive journal-keeper. "Mostly little logistical sorts of stuff that now and then break into writing thoughts, or dreams that may move into songs and back out into something else," he said. "I just like to know where I was and who I was with and what the events were. Also, it comes in handy at tax time—where I was and what I was claiming to be doing."

Butch's journal entry for January 22, 1972, records that, after the band practiced for a couple of nights at the 14th Street house, "I got up late . . . messed around . . . at four o'clock we took off."

He and Joe rode in Butch's venerable VW van, and everyone else piled into Lou D's vehicle. The sun was already declining as they set off down U.S. 87 toward Tahoka, Lamesa, Andrews . . .

Certainly they were curious. The Flatlanders were always nothing if not curious. But were they also excited? Jittery with anticipation? Skeptical that this long car ride, with the cold wind pushing the vehicles around on the blacktop, could yield anything other than a couple of hundred bucks down a rathole?

They'd find out soon enough. Not long after passing through Andrews (which sports two big billboards entering and leaving the town that proclaim "Andrews Supports God, Country and Free Enterprise") and picking up U.S. 385, the lights of Odessa glimmered on the horizon.

The sun was well down by the time Butch's VW van and Country Lou D's automobile pulled into a gravel parking lot at 5600 North Dixie Boulevard, somewhere on the outskirts of town.

It was in the low forties, warm for a West Texas evening in late January. The wind was blowing and kicking up dust—par for the course. Not that there was much to see, dust or no. "There was a house over here and a farm over there," recalled Ely in an NPR interview. "And a pump jack pumping oil over there."

"They were just finishing the ginning so cotton was floating around in the air," Hancock recalled.

The vehicles' headlights picked up what looked like a concrete blockhouse, maybe a meat locker or a similar industrial structure.

"I thought it was somebody's garage," said Steve Wesson.

"We thought it was going to be some piddly little studio," Tony Pearson added.

"It was the only thing for hundreds of yards around. A chunky concrete block building. We all looked around and said, 'So this is a recording studio?' But we got inside and it was actually an amazing place," said Hancock.

"Royce [Clark] knew there was a good studio in Odessa, and we didn't know enough to know a good one from a bad one," Gilmore said. "Unknown to us, it was one of the best studios in the area."

It's easy to understand their skepticism. Finding a first-rate recording studio in a backwater like Odessa in those days would seem to be akin to finding a decent chicken-fried steak in Reykjavik.

(Even today the state's official Texas Music Office lists on its website just one studio in Odessa, and it specializes in Tejano and regional Mexican recordings.)

Odessa was no music mecca. It was and is a scrappy blue-collar oil-field town, famous for its *Friday Night Lights* football mania and a certain pugnacious wadda-you-lookin'-at love/hate relationship with its posher, richer sister city, Midland. The relationship between the two was a rivalry akin to that between Fort Worth and Dallas or the Bronx and Manhattan. Midland and Odessa shared a symphony and chorale, but the nightly soundtrack to Odessa was a lot less Tchaikovsky and a lot more Ernest Tubb. A hotbed of the arts Odessa was not.

But that doesn't take into account Tommy Allsup, who owned the studio that the Flatlanders were examining with such initial skepticism.

Allsup was a big dog in West Texas music. Born in Oklahoma, he set up shop in Odessa in the 1950s because, he said,
"people dance really good in West Texas." His Western Swing
band was renowned enough to attract boogie-woogie hit-maker
Moon Mullican to join up. He played guitar with Buddy Holly
on Holly's last, ill-fated tour, and later with Roy Orbison. He
also played with Holly on Waylon Jennings's first single (produced by Holly). He was a session musician at Norman Petty's
studio in Clovis, New Mexico, and later worked as a producer
in California and Nashville.

He opened his Odessa studio in 1965, and a couple of years
before the Flatlanders turned up he used the room to record a
major Top Ten single, Zagar and Evans's one-hit psychedelic
wonder "In the Year 2525." The room was stocked with the
best outboard gear Allsup could get his hands on, including
a state-of-the-art three-track recording machine like the big
shots in L.A. and New York were using and top-shelf Telefunk-
en mikes (Butch recalled the guys scoffing at this tidbit of info,
not knowing any better; "What the Telefunken?!" and so on).

Of the three-track Ampex recorder, which was popular in
the late sixties, Ely told the Lubbock paper, "I heard later that
Chet Atkins had one, and Capitol Records had three of them.
It's an old-time machine, weighs about 500 pounds with big
old tubes. People like Nat King Cole and Frank Sinatra recorded on them." (Finding one still operating in the twenty-first
century would prove to be the dickens when it came time to
decipher the Odessa recordings.)

Allsup was not there when the group set up to record, and,
sadly, the name of the engineer who ran the session is lost to
history. Which was a pity, because he did an A-list job.

The group set up as they always did, informally in a circle,
and got the ball rolling, playing to one another. Jimmie took
all of the lead vocals (because, Royce Clark wanted a lead

singer to present to Shelby Singleton), with Joe, Butch, and Tony Pearson adding harmonies. Pearson also played mandolin and bass (though the liner notes to *The Odessa Tapes* credit Syl Rice with "string bass 'on some songs'"; Pearson said that was not the case). Joe played Dobro and guitar, Butch added harmonica and guitar. Steve Wesson played the autoharp and his signature musical saw.

"Because of our lack of experience, it made it sound innocent and fresh," said Gilmore.

They recorded pretty much all night, fourteen songs in all. Ten of the tracks, including "Dallas," "Tonight I Think I'm Gonna Go Downtown," and "One Road More," would be reprised in Nashville; four of them—"Number Sixteen," "Shadow of the Moon," "Story of You," and "I Think Too Much of You"— never appeared on any prior Flatlanders recording.

"Somebody punched 'Record' and twelve hours later we walked out of there," said Ely.

Syl Rice and Nubby Mattison and Country Lou D took the master tapes to Nashville to present to Shelby Singleton, which would in turn lead to the Flatlanders' Nashville contract. But before everyone left Odessa, someone dubbed a cassette of the session for the guys to listen to on the way home.

Rolling back toward Lubbock in the early morning light, listening to the cassette through the tinny, two-inch speaker in Butch's van, their hearts fell. It sounded like dogshit.

"It was the worst-quality cassette you ever heard," Hancock said. "Way overrecorded. We couldn't listen to it, it was so bad. There was no way to tell what we had done."

Because they didn't know any better, the Flatlanders thought what they heard on the cassette, static-laden and nearly unlistenable, was all there was. The trip to Odessa had been wasted. A bust. Forget about it and move on.

CHAPTER 8

Now Tennessee is not the state I'm in
And satisfied is not the way I've been

"Tennessee Is Not the State I'm In"
BUTCH HANCOCK

More a Legend

It's hard to know what Shelby Singleton, Jr., was looking for when he offered the Flatlanders (though they were still not known by that moniker) a recording contract with Plantation Records. Its green-labeled 45s were a fixture in truck stops and jukeboxes around the South, and featured a roster of acts like rockabilly stalwart Sleepy LaBeef, a saucy "girl singer" from Texas named Jeannie C. Riley, and country/Cajun star Jimmy Newman. What the Flatlanders might have had in common with these and other Plantation acts was, well, obscure.

"When we first recorded this Flatlanders album, there were, like, five genres in the world, and we had nothing to do with any of them," Joe Ely told a Nashville paper many years later. "It just didn't fit in. It wasn't a country record, and it wasn't a rock record."

But whatever he heard on the Odessa Tapes evidently convinced Singleton there was something there that he could market to country radio.

Singleton died in 2009, but before he passed he reminisced about the band to Richard Gehr. "I thought they were absolutely great," he said. "Their music was strange. Different. Unusual. With the musical saw and Gilmore's vocal style, I thought it stood a chance of being a hit."

"He always liked anything different," said Shelby's brother John, who today is the president of Sun Entertainment Corporation. "He was attracted to a lot of acts that didn't sound like everybody else sounded. He was a gambler, willing to take a chance on an unknown act and see if he could get them played on the radio."

Where the Flatlanders were concerned, that would seem to have been a crapshoot of epic proportions. In 1972, the country charts were dominated by saccharine tripe like Donna Fargo's "The Happiest Girl in the Whole U.S.A.," Tanya Tucker's "Delta Dawn," and Charley Pride's "Kiss an Angel Good Morning." Then there were the harder-edged honky-tonk hits like Buck Owens's "Made in Japan," Mel Tillis's "I Ain't Never," and "Good-Hearted Woman," by the onetime Lubbock deejay Waylon Jennings. The standard-bearers of the Nashville Sound like Tammy Wynette, Lynn Anderson, and Conway Twitty still held fast. Even the Killer himself, Jerry Lee Lewis, was charting again with weepy ballads like "Think About It, Darlin'" and retooled country-flavored versions of his rockabilly hits.

Just where the Flatlanders—with their musical saw, no drums, Gilmore's throwback high-lonesome tenor, and impressionistic, sometimes surreal imagery—were supposed to fit into the commercial Music City matrix is anybody's guess.

One song in their repertoire, "Bhagavan Decreed," by Ed Vizard, a buddy of theirs from Lubbock, mixed Hindu spirituality with Day-Glo hippie duality: "You can burn your brain cells out just trying to get higher / But you'll find the highest place is underground"—not exactly a Grand Ole Opry sing-along.

Ely called their stuff "sort of science-fiction country music. Very strange."

But Singleton—yet another Texan—had a track record of turning out hits. Well before Jeannie C. Riley came into his orbit, Singleton took Bruce Channel's regional Fort Worth crowd-pleaser, "Hey, Baby!" (featuring a young Delbert Mc-Clinton on harmonica), released it on Smash Records, a subsidiary of Mercury Records, where he was employed at the time, and saw it break out as a nationwide pop hit.

A year later, he took another Texas act, Paul and Paula, to the top of the charts with the teenage love song "Hey Paula." He is probably the only executive in Nashville history to produce three Number One records in one day, in sessions with Ray Stevens, Leroy Van Dyke, and Joe Dowell.

He helped enable the careers of not only country artists like Roger Miller, Stevens, and Jerry Reed, but also blues and R&B artists like Ivory Joe Hunter, James Brown, and others. His sessions were often integrated, which was unusual for Nashville at the time.

Producer, musician, and friend Jerry Kennedy told the *Tennessean* newspaper at the time of Singleton's death, "He brought [black artists] like Clyde McPhatter, Brook Benton and Ruth Brown here, and the only hotel where they were allowed to stay was the old Eldorado in North Nashville. So most of the time, the artists stayed with Shelby."

Singleton left Mercury in 1967 and founded his own company with a $1,000 stake. Twenty months later, according to the *Tennessean*, he was worth an estimated $2 million.

"Harper Valley P.T.A." put him on the map. As the story goes, Riley cut the song, and Singleton made an acetate single and took it over to one of the city's marquee disc jockeys, Ralph Emery at WSM. Emery liked it, jumped on it, and thanks to his imprimatur, it was on the way up the charts by morning—a literal overnight success.

Kennedy remembered Singleton as "an all-around record man." At the same time, Singleton was described as "colorful" ... "a maverick" ... "a renegade producer" ... "a character" and "a wheeler-dealer."

There weren't many choirboys on Music Row in those days, and Singleton almost certainly did not number among them.

He couldn't afford to. He was a businessman in a frequently exploitative business that devoured the untutored or the unwary.

Farm boys with stars in their eyes came to Nashville and signed ruinous contracts that stripped them of any publishing and songwriting royalties. Kickbacks between producers and songwriters were common. Managers put their client's name (or their own) as cowriter on a song as a condition of getting it cut, whether the star had ever penned a note or not. (Col. Tom Parker, Elvis Presley's larger-than-life manager, was famous for this not-uncommon practice. He used to ask hungry songwriters who balked at sharing their writer's credit with Elvis, "Do you want 50 percent of something or 100 percent of nothing?")

Payola was not only not dead, it wasn't even sick. In a 1989 ABC News exposé about sharp practices in Nashville, a record promoter seeking to influence disc jockeys to add his clients to their playlists described how it worked: "You brought them [the deejays] to Nashville. They couldn't afford a hotel room and meals, and so we purchased that for them." Other lagniappe could include cruises, new cars, booze, women, or even drugs. One young man named Kevin Hughes, who worked for the trade paper *Cash Box*, was gunned down in a Nashville street in the spring of 1989 when he wouldn't play ball and help rig the *Cash Box* charts.

This was not a ubiquitous state of affairs in Nashville by any means, but it serves as a sort of backdrop to the environment the Flatlanders were fixing to enter, woefully unprepared.

* * *

I been workin' all my life tryin' to beat the company clock
In a Louisiana gravel pit, breakin' up rocks
My baby had enough, she's packin' up and leavin'
She says you're workin' for the man and you ain't breakin' even

"Workin' for the Man"
JOE ELY

———

The Flatlanders, along with Royce Clark and Tommy Hancock, came to Nashville, according to Butch's journal, on March 20, 1972. They arrived in a caravan of sorts, Syl Rice's car and another car belonging to Jimmie's parents.

They entered Singleton Sound Studio and set about getting comfortable. Except for the demo sessions in Odessa, none of them except Clark (and maybe Tommy Hancock) had a lick of experience in the studio.

"When we got to [the studio] they had this big glass room with the engineer in it, and these little booths to separate everybody, with earphones and everything," recalled saw player Steve Wesson. "Intimidating" was probably the right word for the mood.

"The first morning we went over there, it was like ninety dollars an hour, and by about noon everybody was getting pretty tense, because things weren't happening," he continued.

"Finally the engineer said, 'I think I know what's going on.' He came marching out there and started dragging chairs around and got everybody out of the booths and into a circle."

Along in there, with the guys relaxing, playing eye-to-eye, and working out the yips, the Flatlanders, as previously recounted, acquired their name.

"We never played anything the same way twice," Wesson said. "But now we could see each other, so we could key off each other and hear each other. Like we always did, sitting around in a circle and playing. And after he [the engineer] did that, the very next song was a take. And then it was just wham, wham, wham."

At least seventeen songs were keepers: Jimmie's "Dallas" (which Singleton thought might make the first single) and "Tonight I Think I'm Gonna Go Downtown" (written with John X. Reed), the ethereal "Down in My Hometown," and "Not So Long Ago."

Butch was represented with "You've Never Seen Me Cry," the yearning "She Had Everything," "Stars in My Life," and "One Road More," which boasted the sardonic image "I never could move my feet too fast in a pair of rich man's shoes / And there ain't a shoe alive that can last as long as a poor man's blues."

There were two songs by songwriter Al Strehli, "Keeper of the Mountain" and "I Know You" (which boasts one of Jimmie's loveliest vocals), and one by Al's sister, Angela, "The Heart You Left Behind." Angela Strehli would herself go on to great acclaim as a blues singer in Austin and California.

Ed Vizard's "Bhagavan Decreed" made the cut. The set also included "Rose from the Mountain," improbably credited to Louis Driver, aka Country Lou D (on the 2012 release of *The Odessa Tapes*, the same song is credited to one Roy Robinson).

Covers included Willie Nelson's "One Day at a Time," a song whose stoic philosophic outlook fell tongue-in-groove with the Flatlanders' sensibility, along with the Carter Family's "Hello, Stranger" and the Cajun waltz that Harry Choates made a national hit in the mid-1940s, "Jole Blon." Jimmie Rodgers's blue yodel, "Waitin' On a Train," rounded out the set.

The vocals were built around Jimmie Dale Gilmore's well-water-pure voice, although all three shared lead vocal duties back in Lubbock. The idea, as noted, was evidently to market the group as a front man and his band, in the traditional C&W configuration, rather than a group of equals.

Colin Escott, who penned the liner notes for *More A Legend Than A Band*, the 1990 Rounder Records reissue of the Plantation tracks, wrote, "The Flatlanders' sound was akin to a prewar 78 rpm without the crackle and hiss—except that the lyrics were stunningly contemporary. It was a compelling juxtaposition of the old and new; as if Riley Puckett [the blind 1920s-era string band guitarist] had finished a degree in modern poetry and spent a month in the desert with some funny cigarettes."

Despite the success of the recordings and the originality of the performances, there were harbingers of weirdness around the sessions.

"After the sessions, the group was taken out for a photo shoot that did not go as well as had been hoped," Escott continued. "After several abortive experiments, they were taken to the Country Music Hall of Fame and placed in front of the Jimmie Rodgers plaque. 'Then the guy's camera broke,' recalled Gilmore. 'Butch leaned over to me and said, 'Man, Jimmie Rodgers does not want this to happen.'"

Then there was the matter of the Plantation contract.

Not to put too fine a point on it, when it came to the formalities of the corporate music world, the Flatlanders were by and large dumber than a sack of hammers.

"I never signed the contract," said Ely. "I kind of smelled a rat, the way they were talking about it. They never mentioned publishing and things like that."

Thanks to his touring with his bands and as a solo act and his tenures in rough-and-tumble bars and nightclubs (one levied a hundred-dollar cover charge on potential black patrons, and Joe had at least one gun pulled on him by a club owner), Ely was a little more savvy about the unsavory side of the business. But only a little.

"When we got there, they said, 'We want to sign you [as a solo artist], or sign the band," said Gilmore. "Whichever way you want to do it. And I said to Joe, 'I'll sign a deal for the band if you will.' And Joe said, 'No, I don't want to sign it.'

"Joe wanted to do rock and roll, and he didn't necessarily want to be stuck [in the acoustic direction the Flatlanders were headed]. But he did like being a part of it.

"Plus, it was more my thing we were doing. Royce had asked for a tape with me [doing all the lead vocals]. That was kind of stupid in itself in retrospect. It sort of missed the point of what we were doing."

The bottom line was, the band had no one looking exclusively after *its* interests.

"So I signed it," Gilmore said. "Lou had become my manager. I don't know if that was a mistake or not. But what else was there to do? He knew more about the business than anybody we knew. Anybody else in Lubbock would have been the same as him. And what he did was, he sold us out to them. I didn't ever knowingly sign anything that gave my publishing rights to Plantation or Shelby Singleton."

Publishing on the Flatlanders' original material was split between two companies, Prize and Urn. Prize was registered to John Singleton through ASCAP. Urn was co-owned by Lou Driver and Royce Clark.

So "Jimmy [sic] Dale and the Flatlanders" became Plantation Records recording artists. There was a new album in the can, to be called *All American Music*.

Now it was time for Shelby Singleton to work his record-man mojo.

In April, "Dallas" was to be the first single, and, just as he had with Jeannie C. Riley, Singleton planned to follow the time-tested process of getting the record into the hands of a nationally known, taste-making deejay who could jump-start the single up the charts.

The disc jockey in this case was Bill Mack, "The Midnight Cowboy," an alumnus of KDAV in Lubbock, as it happened, who had gone on to host the nightly *Country Roads Show* on WBAP in Dallas/Fort Worth. The big clear-channel station beamed Mack's distinctive voice across most of the country, and he became a favorite of all-night truckers who would radio in dedications, messages to loved ones, and the latest truckers' gossip. He was also a hit-making songwriter in his own right, having penned "Drinkin' Champagne," which became a hit for Cal Smith and, later, George Strait. His 1997 song, "Blue," helped put LeAnn Rimes on the map. Mack was just the guy, Singleton figured, to help launch his fellow Texans onto the national scene.

But it wasn't meant to be. Mack took one listen to the song's dark lyrics—"Dallas is a woman who will walk on you when you're down / Dallas ain't a woman to help you get your feet on the ground . . . Dallas is a rich man with a death wish in his eye / A rich man who tends to believe in his own lies"—and turned thumbs down.

"Royce Clark told me that Bill Mack said the song 'belittled the city,'" said Gilmore years later. And that was that.

Gilmore recalled the song became Number One at a radio station in, he thinks, Colorado Springs. And Lloyd Maines contends that the guys' rendition of the Cajun classic "Jole Blon" got into regular rotation at KLLL in Lubbock.

But as far as Shelby Singleton was concerned, it was time to cut his losses. "In those years," he said to Richard Gehr, "we didn't release albums unless we could market them."

He ran off a small quantity of the album on eight-track tapes and let the whole project slide quietly into oblivion.

Many years later, Ely claimed he got ahold of some of the eight-tracks with Flatlanders cover art, but when he plugged one in, Jeannie C. Riley's voice came out of the speakers.

As for the Flatlanders, they went home to Texas and waited for . . . whatever.

"That summer, we went traveling around and we were thinking, the record's gonna be coming out any day," Gilmore said. "And slowly, through the rest of the year, we figured out, aw, these guys aren't doing anything. I don't remember specifically when, but I do remember coming upon the realization that nothing was happening."

Jimmie reckoned the Nashville suits weren't really into a serious vision of the Flatlanders' potential. "They knew there was something interesting about this band, but they perceived us as kind of a novelty group, like we were from *Hee-Haw* or something," he recounted in *Lubbock Lights*.

And then there was the matter of the money—there wasn't any.

To this day, they contend, they have not received any returns from the Nashville sessions—no session pay, no songwriters' royalties, no mechanical royalties (which are based on record sales), no airplay royalties. This, despite the tracks having been released overseas in 1980 (as *One Road More* on the Charly label) and in the United States in 1990 (as *More A Legend Than A Band*, on Rounder Records) and in 1995 (as *"Unplugged"* on Singleton's Sun Records).

"Not a penny," says Ely today. "Butch and Jimmie never saw a penny from publishing or a royalty check even though they wound up licensing it to Europe twice and to Rounder. I understand that when it was released in Europe it sold over 100,000 copies. And Rounder sold a lot here too, but we've never gotten an accounting or anything on it."

According to Rounder cofounder Bill Nowlin, by the end of the first royalty period, in March 1990, the album had sold 3,234 copies, and based on the royalty rate at the time, the label issued a check for $1,743.40. By 2005, the most recent period to which Nowlin had ready access, the album had sold more than 20,000 copies.

"We went and made the record without getting paid a penny," Gilmore said. "My dad loaned us his car and paid for gas."

"I think it's correct that they were badly treated during the process," said Mike Tolleson, an Austin entertainment lawyer who is looking into reclaiming the publishing rights to Butch's and Jimmie's songs.

Without seeing the contract and talking to the principals, of course, I can't say if the Flatlanders were intentionally victimized by Shelby Singleton, Royce Clark, and Lou Driver, or if, in their naïveté, they simply signed a hard-nosed but legitimate contract without being aware of its far-reaching implications.

Neither Shelby Singleton nor (so far as I've been able to discover) Clark nor Driver is around to give his account of events.

John Singleton asserted that nothing underhanded occurred. At the time the Flatlanders were signed, he was in charge of Business Affairs at Sun, which included negotiating contracts.

"I don't recall all the details," he said. "But what I recall was, they agreed to do the sessions on sort of a spec deal, and if we liked it, we'd put the record out. But I don't know if there was any agreement to actually pay them to do the sessions, since they would benefit from having a record out as much or more than we would."

As to the publishing winding up in the Prize/Urn catalogs, he said, "I think the artist contract had a clause in it stating that if they recorded a song that they wrote, then we had the right to publish it, what they call a Control of Copyright clause."

As to royalties, he conceded, "We probably do still owe them some royalty statements, but it would be very minimal."

Whatever the case, it is ironic that the musical legacy on which the Flatlanders' decades-long, international reputation rests never recouped a proverbial nickel for its creators.

"We have to look at it like, it was great that the music exists, because we can't go back and be bitter," Ely says now.

Years later, with his producer's ear having been honed by experience, Ely went back and listened to the Nashville tracks and determined that Singleton or producer Royce Clark—or someone—had overdubbed additional session musicians onto the group's tracks without telling them.

"I realized that someone had come in and put on an acoustic guitar part to try to straighten out our sloppiness. They overdubbed parts on top to try to thicken it up."

In 1990, when Rounder was preparing to release thirteen of the seventeen tracks as *More A Legend Than A Band*, the guys reached out to Singleton's office with a request to remix the album themselves before Rounder got the tracks, only to be told the master tapes had been destroyed. The tracks that exist on record as they are today, overdubs and all, are the only permanent record of the Flatlanders' Nashville foray.

Still, the album holds up, lo these forty-plus years later. *No Depression* magazine, in 2000, said the Nashville recordings "enjoy an enduring and undeniable mystique. Evoking the wind-swept plains and endless horizon of the Texas Panhandle, as well as the feelings of isolation that went with living there—alienation that Ely likens to being 'in a concentration camp on the moon'—the record brilliantly captured both the band's geographic and social location."

Talking Heads founder David Byrne, a longtime friend and admirer of Lubbock's musical Mafia, thought the album was great and cited the Flatlanders' influence. "I loved it, the reissue of their record," he told filmmaker Amy Maner in *Lubbock Lights*. "It was for Texas music what the Velvet Underground was for New York. It was a group that didn't sell any records, but as someone said, everyone who heard the record started a band and began writing songs."

"The album's got a lonesome, West Texas quality—Jimmie's high-lonesome moan, my terrible Dobro playing, a saw playing through the whole thing," says Ely. "It sounds like flying saucers landing. You couldn't copy it if you tried."

"It's an amazingly weird little album," says Hancock. "It's real listenable after all these years. It's got that West Texas atmosphere in there. You can kind of hear the air and the wind in there somewhere. The thing has almost been a missing link in the music world."

Indeed. The Flatlanders didn't invent Americana or alt-country or the Texas singer/songwriter tradition, but their work, as well as the solo work of the three principals, casts a long shadow over the performers and genres that have arisen since their journey to Nashville. Robert Earl Keen, the Cowboy Junkies, Ryan Bingham, Terry Allen, John Hiatt, Hayes Carll, Lucinda Williams, Steve Earle, Lyle Lovett—make up your own list. All of them and more have been informed, perhaps overtly, perhaps subconsciously, by the music these West Texans made (and continue to make).

As spring and summer gave way to autumn, the band meandered around Texas. They played the first Kerrville Folk Festival (more on that later) and established a foothold in Austin, playing the Armadillo World Headquarters beer garden and some local honky-tonks. They played a festival in Victoria and a few other places, but there was no wind in their sails.

Sometime, somewhere, in the waning months of 1972—maybe at the Armadillo, maybe in some living room in Lubbock, no one knows exactly where—the original incarnation of the Flatlanders played their last gig.

CHAPTER 9

There's a lot of water under the bridges
That are burning
But it's a fact we can finally float or fly just fine

"Outside the Lines"
JIMMIE DALE GILMORE

Diaspora

In retrospect, it's easy to see how it all could have been different.

Country music is an industry that has historically looked inward, not outward. Things are done because, well, that's the way they've always been done. The larger popular culture—its evolving trends and mutating ways of doing business—is largely ignored or, at most, grudgingly accommodated. Today's country stars (or minions acting in their name) text, Tweet, and Facebook-post with abandon, it's true. But at the end of the day, press-the-flesh audience interactions like Fan Fair, radio play and corresponding hit singles, and corporate top-down management still rule the roost in Music City, long after the rest of the music business has moved on to multiplatform social media, streaming content, and DIY indie innovation.

That insular attitude was as dominant in 1972 as it is today. If, instead of trying to cater to country radio's bigwigs as he'd always done, Singleton had looked out to see what was going on in Los Angeles, San Francisco, New York, Boston, Ann Arbor, and Austin, he might have pitched the Flatlanders very differently, and with much greater success.

Out on the Left and Right Coasts, in Texas and in university towns and other enclaves, musicians, college radio stations, and underground FM stations were rewriting the rules by which musical genres nudged up against each other and cross-pollinated.

Meanwhile, musicians like Gram Parsons (both with the Flying Burrito Bros. and on his own), Poco, Buffalo Springfield, the Nitty Gritty Dirt Band, and Bob Dylan in his *John Wesley Harding/Nashville Skyline* phase were mixing country, folk, and rock in new and liberating ways. It was the era of the Byrds' *Sweetheart of the Rodeo* and the Rolling Stones' "Country Honk" and "Wild Horses."

If the Flatlanders had been pointed at a hip young college audience instead of Bill Mack's late-night, pill-popping, long-haul truckers . . . or if Shelby Singleton had sold the album to a cooler, more dialed-in label like Warner Bros., Vanguard, Elektra, or A&M, their story might have had a happier ending.

But the Flatlanders were victims of Nashville's creative myopia and their own naïveté.

"We didn't know enough to complain about not making it [the marketing effort] more broad-ranging," said Jimmie Dale Gilmore in *Lubbock Lights*. "They should have presented us to the San Francisco and New York audiences [versus mainstream country radio]. It was totally the wrong time for that. They thought we were a country band, which we were, but not commercial country."

As he told Christopher Oglesby, "On the other hand, we weren't really particularly ambitious to begin with. We weren't trying to do anything big and huge or anything. It was just fun;

we did it for fun. After we recorded it, there was this period where we went, 'Oh, boy! We'll sell millions!' But it wasn't why the band was put together to begin with. So it was a fluke that this even happened.

"I decided a really long time ago I wasn't going to flip out and be angry forever. What's the point?"

Maybe, looking back, the high point of the whole exercise might have been when the Flatlanders were driving back to Texas from Nashville in Jimmie's dad's car and heard Bill Mack giving "Dallas" one of its rare spins on WBAP.

If Shelby Singleton was stuck in Nashville wearing bifocals, the Flatlanders had twenty-twenty vision in Austin. The new alchemy was happening right before their eyes. Artists like Jerry Jeff Walker, Michael Martin Murphey, Asleep at the Wheel, Greezy Wheels, Freda and the Firedogs (featuring piano prodigy Marcia Ball), and, above all, Willie Nelson were throwing out the rulebook, mixing up the hippies and the rednecks, and creating a new musical fusion and a new audience all at once.

Austin in the early seventies was every bit as hip, under-the-radar, and laid-back as the old farts who were there in the day like to yammer on and on about (Your Humble Author stands guilty as charged).

Novelist and screenwriter Bud Shrake called it "the hippie Palm Springs." Tex-Mex rocker Doug Sahm, who'd sampled the high life in San Francisco and Amsterdam and who'd once had the Rolling Stones open for *him*, dubbed the town "Groover's Paradise."

The reasons were at once complex and simple.

Complex in the sense that a sociologist might generate many acres of graphs and pie charts and theses out of the social, political, sexual, and economic interaction among the enormous student population at the University of Texas, the young legislators and the aides and lobbyists who came to the

Texas Capitol (and who often felt free to frolic, far from their conservative constituents), and the flyboys at the local air force base with lots of time and money on their hands.

Simple in the sense that the Hill Country landscape was physically beautiful (especially if you were coming from West Texas), a cadre of friends could rent a house for about seventy bucks a month, sloe-eyed hippie girls sunbathed topless at the city's beloved Barton Springs pool, music was everywhere, and pot was for many, many years just ten dollars an ounce.

Songwriter Steve Earle left town for Nashville, explaining that the Texas capital had way too many pretty girls and way too much cheap dope to get any work done.

Austin had, in the words of novelist Billy Lee Brammer, "room enough to caper."

The cliché was and is that Austin is the blue liberal island in the red ocean that is conservative Texas, and there is some truth to that.

Eddie Wilson took one look at these three skinny West Texas ex-pats and got it from the get-go.

"The Flatlanders were the coolest guy in the room, the most diverse guy in the room, and the most sincere guy in the room. And anybody could tell which one was which," he said.

"They were so stupefying for the simple fact that they were perfect from Day One. The two greatest things were that saw and the fact of no drummer—there was something incredibly authentic about this bunch. And then, the material was unbelievable. The intelligence level was so fucking progressive."

Wilson, you'll recall, was the guy pissing against the wall with (so it's said) Jimmie and guitarist John X. Reed on either side of him when he had his "Eureka!" moment that led to the opening of the Armadillo World Headquarters.

Wilson knew Gilmore through his band, the Hub City Movers, who would play on the Armadillo's opening night bill. He knew Ely by proxy, because Ely hooked up with Wilson's buddy,

Austin artist Jim Franklin (who would become the Armadillo's artist-in-residence), to go to New York and then on to Europe with an Austin theater troupe. So there was a certain familiarity on his part with these Lubbock guys.

It made sense for him to put the Flatlanders in the Armadillo's new outdoor beer garden and in the big room as circumstances permitted. (One poster on Wilson's wall is an October 1972 'Dillo calendar putting the band both in the beer garden midweek, billed as "The Texas Flatlanders," and then opening for Freda and the Firedogs as "The Flatlanders" on the main stage on Saturday night. Admission was a buck.) A decade later, they returned to play at the big blowout when the Armadillo turned out the lights for good on December 30–31, 1980.

It's hard to imagine the Armadillo arising anywhere else in Texas. Presenting acts that ranged from Frank Zappa to Bill Monroe, Van Morrison to Fats Domino, Waylon Jennings to ZZ Top, the venue was all about slicing, dicing, and blending musical genres. Bruce Springsteen played the room when he was just a scrappy Jersey rocker testing the waters outside the Right Coast. A local Western Swing fiddle player named Alvin Crow opened up for him. The audience dug 'em both.

Willie Nelson chose the Armadillo to make his mainstream Austin debut one hot August night in 1972 after moving back to the Lone Star capital for good. He deliberately threw the 'Dillo's long-haired, pot-smoking regulars in with his traditional Pearl Beer–drinking audience of rednecks and cedar choppers. Some questioned his sanity and feared a riot.

"I knew all along that kids would respond to what we were doing," he said years later, after the show was a roaring success. "And my band knew that I knew, so they weren't worried. But my booking agent thought I was crazy, and so did the industry people in New York and L.A. and Nashville. But they didn't know what we did, they never got out of their offices to check out what was happening."

That was the audience Shelby Singleton should have been chasing.

That was the audience that responded to what the Flatlanders had to offer. Just witness the reception they received when they wandered into the first Kerrville Folk Festival in June 1972.

Like so much else in the Flatlanders saga, it was a fluke and yet another chorus of "nothin' else to do."

According to Steve Wesson, the guys had a friend named T. J. Nabors. "She was a weaver and we went down mostly to see the festival and to see her," he said. "We didn't have much money, so we just set up in front of her booth and put a guitar case out there and started playing. Her boyfriend, Bobby Elkins, was a filmmaker (making a documentary on the festival) and he filmed us." Some of that footage, featuring the guys performing "Stars in My Life," can be seen in Amy Maner and George Sledge's *Lubbock Lights*.

Going on forty-three years, the Kerrville Folk Festival is held each spring at an outdoor site nine miles south of Kerrville, the graceful Hill Country town on the Guadalupe River. But for the first two years of its existence, the festival found an indoor home at the Kerrville Municipal Auditorium. Then, as now, the festival is congruent with the Texas State Arts and Crafts Fair, which was where Nabors had a booth and where the Flatlanders set up shop.

"People started hollering for the Flatlanders," Tony Pearson said. "So they started putting us on the (festival) venues every day. We followed (East Texas country bluesman) Mance Lipscomb once."

Hancock continued, "So we were just down there playing under a tree at the fairground when (festival founder) Rod Kennedy and Peter Yarrow (of Peter, Paul and Mary fame) wandered by and heard us and said, 'Hey, you should come over to the Festival and play at the New Folk songwriters' contest. So we went over and signed up and I think we were twenty-sixth on the list.

Janette Norman recalled that Yarrow became a staunch advocate for the guys on the spot.

"I think we played 'Dallas' and Peter Yarrow came running up to the stage and said, 'Hey, we gotta get you guys to come up and play on my set tonight at the Auditorium.' We thought we had made the big time. Though we still had to pay for our girlfriends to get in."

In a sense, they *had* made the big time. It was by far the largest crowd they'd ever played for. Former president Lyndon B. Johnson had retired after the 1968 election to his sprawling ranch near Johnson City—not so far away from Kerrville as the crow flies in the Texas Hill Country. Since leaving the Oval Office he had been relaxing and letting his hair down, literally. Photos from the era show him with a silvery mane almost as long as what the hippies he once disdained wore.

Johnson, his wife Lady Bird, and UT football coach Darrell K Royal decided to motor over to Kerrville to catch this new music festival everyone was talking about.

So there were the Flatlanders, onstage, playing a few feet from the not-so-former Leader of the Free World.

That was a hard moment to top, though one wonders what Ely, who had participated in antiwar rallies in Lubbock, might have said to LBJ in a private moment.

The Flatlanders took themselves back to Austin after Kerrville concluded. There was a comfort level present in the city engendered in part by a supportive community of West Texans lured by the local amenities—Trees! Rivers! Beer!—and the growing creative community as a whole.

"It was literally one of those godsends," said Eddie Wilson, never prone to understatement, speaking of the musical and artistic ignition that took place in the early 1970s.

"It was like, a clap of thunder and everybody moved here. They were getting away from something and getting into something, and what they got into they created by coming here."

The Flatlanders weren't so much caught up in that current of creativity as they were swirling in an eddy, watching it flow by without plunging in. With no record on the horizon and no prospect of making another one, and little initiative ("We didn't have a thimbleful of ambition. . . . We were doing it for fun") to forge a career as a unit, the band members were spectators, not stakeholders.

Forces were already conspiring to pull them in different directions: Butch up to the Panhandle and to Clarendon, Jimmie Dale to New Orleans and then Colorado, Ely to the East Coast and New York City, Steve and Tony to New Mexico . . .

Butch's and Jimmie's and Joe's individual journeys in music were just about to begin. Suddenly, the Flatlanders were in the rearview mirror.

"The day they pulled into Austin after Nashville, they came to the Armadillo and I can still remember them sitting on the floor of my office. I don't even know if they had a place to stay," said Mike Tolleson, who was one of Wilson's partners in the 'Dillo.

"They were all excited about the record and thinking it was going to come out at some point soon. And they went out and played in the beer garden and everybody loved 'em. I don't think anybody had ever seen a band with a saw in it before. That got people's attention. They were welcome to stay around and play as much as they wanted to.

"I learned later that they went to Kerrville and then came back here and played the Split Rail and the One Knite and made those rounds. Then I sort of go blank. It's almost as if they went back to Lubbock and disappeared."

PART FOUR

The Men,
Second Verse

*Everything's changed but the wildness of our
hearts and the beauty of those songs*

"When We Were All Bluebirds"
MICHAEL VENTURA

CHAPTER 10

There's two kinds of people in this big ol' town
That's the early to rise and the late to go down
I guess I better find another way to stop the clock
Hot dawg, I LIKE IT A LOT!

"Musta Notta Gotta Lotta"
JOE ELY

Joe, Jimmie, and Butch, Part 2

Terry Allen was talking one day from his home in Santa Fe. "There's two people that I think are really great stage performers, and they're both shy," he was saying. "And that's Joe and [Talking Heads frontman] David Byrne.

"From the time that I met both of them and had any occasion to be in a kitchen or a living room where they're playing you a song, the intensity of it is the same in that kitchen as it is onstage. Whenever they play a song for you, they play all of it, and they put all of themselves into it.

"Joe is completely restless. It's almost like the stage is kind of a cage for him. Normally, he would be out going a hundred miles an hour in a car, or going from one pool hall to another. Somehow on stage, that energy is confined and it comes out in that music."

"That music" first manifested itself on an autumn night in Lubbock in 1974 when Ely was tapped by the owners of the Main Street Saloon, near the Tech campus, to fill in an empty weekend slot that arose suddenly after a band cancellation.

"We noticed this guy come in and kinda walk around in a Barnum & Bailey circus jumpsuit," said Main Street Saloon co-owner Bruce Jaggers in Oglesby's *Fire in the Water, Earth in the Air*.

"And this guy says, 'Hey, I'm a musician. I can put together a band for you.' We did not know him at all. I didn't grow up in Lubbock, and I'd never heard of the Flatlanders. So we were like, 'Well, we don't have anybody else. That sounds good.' And it was Joe Ely." Jaggers had no idea that Ely had been downing endless cups of coffee at Broadway Drugs, scheming ways and means to put another band together at long last.

Ely was trying to move to Austin, where the local progressive country scene was firing on all cylinders, but he needed some traveling money. A weekend pickup gig should get him down the road. He called Lloyd Maines (whom he knew through Caldwell Studios) to play pedal steel, a guitarist named Rick Hulett, and a bass player, Gregg Wright, to fill in the date. A one-off band for a one-off show. No drummer.

Jaggers and his partner, John Kenyon, didn't know what they had in Ely. Probably Ely didn't know himself. He'd spent the last several years traveling as a solo busker with his guitar slung over his shoulder, and he'd been part of the acoustic/folk/country Flatlanders troika. But this was a honky-tonk Saturday night crowd, and acoustic balladry wasn't going to cut it.

That night, Joe Ely reached inside and found the onstage incarnation that would last him a lifetime.

"It was unrehearsed; we just did a bunch of Hank Williams and Jimmie Rodgers songs, and some Butch, Jimmie, and Ely originals," said Maines. "And the crowd went absolutely nuts."

The next weekend, said Maines, "the line to get in the place was lined all the way down University Avenue." Suddenly, moving to Austin just didn't seem so urgent. "Joe started to think, 'I'll stay here for a while and ride this out and see where it goes.'"

Ely had the hottest band in town, even without a drummer. Maines described Ely and the electricity onstage as "riveting." The group finally enlisted Steve Keeton to play drums when they had the opportunity to play a big show at the Municipal Auditorium, opening for country-rocker B. W. Stevenson.

Before long the band was packing in crowds at local watering holes like Fat Dawg's, Coldwater Country, and the Cotton Club—doing original songs, no less, in an environment that mostly rewarded familiar cover songs.

A rocker at heart, Ely was on the verge of having the band he'd always heard in his head. "Even in junior high I'd always been leaning toward having a loud band," he told Don McLeese. "There was something I liked about having the neighbors slam the door and call the cops."

More than adding a drummer, though, what transformed the Joe Ely Band into a weapons-grade honky-tonk band was a barrel-chested blues-rock guitarist named Jesse Taylor.

Rick Hulett, the band's original guitarist, had left, and along comes this guy with the apt nickname of "Hercules."

Taylor looked like something out of a cartoon, with a long-shoreman's face under a black pompadour, a hulking torso, and skinny Yosemite Sam legs. Though he looked like he could break you over his knee, Jesse Taylor was in reality funny, philosophical, and sweet-tempered—most of the time—and a voracious reader with a soft, almost whispery voice.

When he and Lloyd Maines first began to rehearse together with Ely, it was obvious something was in the air.

Maines was from local country music royalty. His father and uncles had formed the original Maines Brothers Band in the 1950s and 1960s. As kids, Lloyd and the younger boys performed as the "Little Maines Brothers," before donning the Maines Brothers Band moniker themselves in the 1970s. Lloyd was also an engineer and in-house steel guitarist at Don Caldwell's studio, where Ely would record his first demo.

A pedal steel guitar is typically the sentimental, weeping counterpoint to a country vocalist who's singing about hard luck and trouble. But when he and Jesse teamed up onstage with Ely, Lloyd's steel was suddenly a keening, wailing engine that could roar like a jet afterburner or howl like a runaway freight. Taylor drove him on, throwing off one muscular solo after another, while Maines responded in furious kind.

The Allman Brothers had done some pioneering work with harmony guitars, but there never had been (and still hasn't been) anything quite like Jesse and Lloyd's combustible interplay.

Listen to "Boxcars" or "Johnny Blues" off of Ely's debut album and there is still, thirty-seven years after its release, an eye-opening intensity to the fiery exchanges between the two guitarists.

"I played over a thousand shows with Jesse to my left," said Maines. "I think back, how lucky I was to hear the magic coming out of his amp. He would reinvent himself every night." Taylor died before his time in 2006.

Little more than a year after Ely sat drinking coffee in Broadway Drugs and resolving to at last put a band together, he had a contract with MCA Records' Nashville division.

With Lloyd's help, Ely recorded a demo at Caldwell Studios. Ely's manager, Johnny Hughes, dubbed some cassette copies, one of which he gave to Bob Livingston, a fellow Lubbockite. Livingston, as it happened, played bass for Jerry Jeff Walker, who was MCA's biggest Texas star at the moment.

Livingston played the tape for a gaggle of MCA execs and told them how to get in touch with Hughes and Ely. After they saw a pair of shows, one at the Cotton Club ("It was one of those Cotton Club nights when everybody was sweaty and the crowd was just seething," recalled Lloyd) and one at Austin's Split Rail beer joint (which Hughes and Butch Hancock arranged), the label signed the band. His debut album, *Joe Ely*, was released in 1977.

Which was great, as far as it went.

Almost immediately a problem reared its head that would persist throughout Ely's long on-again, off-again history with MCA and his other labels: They didn't have a clue how to market him successfully. Too rock for country radio, too country for rock stations outside of Texas.

When Ely added accordionist Ponty Bone to the mix to lend a spicy Cajun/Tex-Mex punch to the sound, and later hired sax players Smokey Joe Miller and Bobby Keys, and layered on soul-style keyboards (by Reese Wynans, who would later hire on with Stevie Ray Vaughan), it just muddied the waters further.

"I'll never forget playing a song in 1977 for one of those big Nashville stations, WSM I think, with an accordion on it, and having this guy tell me, 'You can't have an accordion on a Nashville record,'" he said to *Dirty Linen*.

(One time, after Ely recorded a lovely song called "Love Is the Beating of Hearts," his A-list Nashville producer Tony Brown turned to him and said, "Maybe we shouldn't do this, Joe—this might appeal to the masses and ruin everything.")

As if that wasn't enough, he struck up an improbable friendship with Joe Strummer and the other members of the Clash, who came to see the band in 1978, when Ely was touring the U.K. They became instant mutual fans.

"It was the West Texas hell-raisers meets the London hell-raisers," Ely told the *Austin Chronicle*. Ely offered to put together a Texas tour of out-of-the-way venues in exotic-sounding locales the band was fascinated by. "A promoter's nightmare," Ely chuckled, citing dates in Laredo, Lubbock, and Wichita Falls.

Strummer invited Ely back to England in 1980 to play dates with the Clash during the *London Calling* tour. "Playing with the Clash definitely kicked my band up a notch," Ely added.

Though he never bought into the band's radical political stance, the Clash's punkish energy inspired Ely to drive his own ensemble even harder.

Nonstop touring (Ely once sent his booking agent a highway map for Christmas as a protest) and nonstop, balls-out musical intensity and personal excesses by some members shattered Ely's first great band as 1983 dawned, but by then his reputation as a great live performer was cemented.

Ely never came close to having a radio hit, although he eventually opened shows for Linda Ronstadt, Tom Petty, and even the Rolling Stones. In the ironic words of one of his own songs, he was driving to the poorhouse in a limousine.

But his fan base word-of-mouth wasn't based on radio play. Folks came out to see Ely because he could melt down a stage.

Here's my own stab, circa 1982 or so, at describing the phenomenon: "In those early years, Ely was all over the stage, ricocheting from the speaker stacks to the drum kit, bouncing off the bass player, winding up with the toes of his cowboy boots hooked over the lip of the stage as his body vibrated like a human question mark. Sweat streaming, arms flailing, singing about open roads and backstreet girls, Ely jumped like a cat in a roomful of rocking chairs."

Once in the early eighties, I was in the audience when Ely was playing the Kerrville Folk Festival. A thunderstorm rolled in and a lightning strike killed almost all the power at the outdoor site. Ely was onstage and managed to plug a microphone into his old Super Reverb amp and keep playing. The rain was falling in buckets, thunder crashing, lightning licking down.

Ely was courting electrocution with every note, howling back into the eye of the storm: "I'm a-gonna tell you how it's gonna be! / You're gonna give your love to me!" Buddy Holly's "Not Fade Away," what else? It was deranged, it was breathtaking, and it was unforgettable.

He had the onstage swagger and the offstage charisma—if you saw him across a crowded airport lobby, you might not know who he was, but he looked like he *ought* to be somebody. His lean frame, with a shock of tangled black hair and piercing dark eyes, sometimes seemed to resonate with energy. The cowboy boots, bolo tie, and Ray-Ban shades just reinforced the image. Even without seeing the gig bag with the electric guitar inside slung over his shoulder, you knew the road and the stage were his natural habitats.

Even though today he qualifies for Social Security, Ely is still a riveting performer to watch, leaning into the mike to sing, peering out into the dark with those black Indian eyes, and slashing with the neck of his guitar, as though it were a scythe, at a song's conclusion.

Writing under a 1981 headline, "Guitar Festival Reaps a Whirlwind," prestigious *Los Angeles Times* critic Robert Hilburn described the Joe Ely Band cutting a swath through a genteel San Diego acoustic music festival: "The real news, however, was Joe Ely, a Texas country-rocker who was . . . dazzling. Ely's six-piece group played with enough fury to TKO Bruce Springsteen's E-Street Band. . . . Ely reached out to the crowd so eagerly at times it looked as if he was going to fall off the 10-foot stage. . . . Ely expands our concept of 'country rock' by making exciting and original music that lives up to the best traditions of both styles. No once since the late Gram Parsons has shown so much purity and heart in dealing with both styles."

Thirty years later, another L.A. reviewer said of him, "Once you've seen him perform you know you've experienced something unique, original and legendary."

Given that lifelong commitment to uncompromising performance, it's no surprise that the albums that best reflect that legacy are the live recordings Ely cuts every decade or so: *Live Shots* (1980), *Live at Liberty Lunch* (1990), *Live @ Antones* (2000), *Live Chicago 1987*, and *Live Cactus* (the last two 2008).

Each is designed to commemorate a certain era and a certain sound. *Live Shots* is that first Ely band at the peak of its white-hot intensity, recorded while on tour with the Clash in England. *Live at Liberty Lunch*, recorded at a late-lamented Austin club, is a showcase for his second great ensemble, a tough little quartet that included guitarist David Grissom, drummer Davis McLarty, and bassist Jimmy Pettit.

Live @ Antones marks a reunion of Maines and Taylor on steel and guitar, but it also features flamenco guitarist Teye, who toured with Ely for several years and reflected his longtime fascination with Mexican, Spanish, flamenco, and gypsy melodies. *Live Cactus*, recorded at Austin's acoustic listening room the Cactus Café, is a more subdued and intimate affair, featuring just Ely and accordionist Joel Guzman. *Live Chicago 1987* chronicles a particularly hot night onstage and features fellow West Texan Bobby Keys on tenor sax.

Ely has made a fistful of great studio albums, of course. My personal list would include his debut, his second recording, *Honky Tonk Masquerade* (1978), the hard-rocking *Musta Notta Gotta Lotta* (1981), *Love and Danger* (1992), the Tex-Mex-flavored *Letter to Laredo* (1995), which features a guest vocal by Ely fan Bruce Springsteen on the great "All Just to Get to You," and his latest, as of this writing, *Satisfied at Last* (2011).

Also worthy of mention is the maligned-in-its-day curiosity *Hi-Res* (1984). An early adopter of tech, especially computers, Ely did the original tracks for the whole album on an Apple

II computer. It might have been the first pop record using that method—high tech in its day, laughably antiquated now. Nevertheless, it was too avant-garde for MCA, which made Ely re-record the album with "real" musicians, including members of the Austin jazz-rock fusion group Passenger.

Fans scratched their heads at the time, but much of the album holds up well over time, and *Hi-Res* includes such future Ely anthems as "Cool Rockin' Loretta," "Letter to Laredo," and "She Gotta Get the Gettin'."

Ely moved to Austin for keeps in 1980 and married Sharon in 1982; the two had a daughter, Marie Elena (named after Buddy Holly's widow), the following year. By then, Ely had become disenchanted with his hometown. After fans trampled the buffalo grass turf in Buddy Holly Park during Ely's third Tornado Jam festival in 1983, the city council banned live music in the venue.

Ely had conceived of the Tornado Jams as a tribute to the never-say-die resilience of Lubbockites in the wake of the devastating 1970 cyclone, but the city's ongoing indifference to the music and musicians who put the city on the map, and its tone-deaf sensibility in kicking live music out of Buddy Holly Park—of all places!—pissed him off.

Like most of the musicians and artists who come out of there, Ely remains conflicted about his hometown and West Texas.

"When you grew up there," he told *Texas Monthly* in 2000, "you realized that isn't where you wanted to be, especially if you had actually gotten out of there and seen the world."

And yet, when it comes time to write a new batch of songs (not that he's ever *not* writing), he's apt to jump in his car and take off for the Panhandle, driving the empty grid of remote farm-to-market dirt roads out between, say, Clarendon and Quitaque, soaking up the sky and the silence and the space. It is, he says, regenerative:

"It's a blank canvas, and also a big, huge empty space to fill. And there's nothing like a song to fill up a big empty space."

His last major label album was 1998's *Twistin' in the Wind*, for MCA Nashville. Two more discs for Rounder Records followed, *Live @ Antones* and *Streets of Sin* (2003), the latter of which contains a lyric that marks the miles since a young Joey Ely started riding his thumb with his hopes up high: "The dogs go to barkin' / At the risin' of the moon / And the highway's a-callin' / I'll be listenin' soon / Another weary rambler / Crazy as a loon."

Ely put the established record labels in his rearview mirror for keeps and formed his own imprint, Rack 'Em Records, in 2007. It only made sense; he already had his own recording studio in a building adjoining his Hill Country stone ranch house, and he'd learned enough about the business to know his musical vision transcended corporate pigeonholes.

Besides, thanks to the Internet, by the middle of the century's first decade the traditional record industry model was melting away like a Popsicle on Hell's own sidewalk.

In keeping with his peripatetic, eternally restless nature, he jumped into the DIY pond with both cowboy-booted feet. In early 2007 he not only released a disc of new material, *Happy Songs from Rattlesnake Gulch*, but also a book for the University of Texas Press, *Bonfire of Roadmaps*, a sometimes surreal, almost open verse/stream-of-consciousness travelogue taken from the back-pocket journals he'd been keeping for decades.

Simultaneously, he released a two-man acoustic album (with accordionist Joel Guzman) entitled *Silver City*, comprising new recordings of old songs he had, for the most part, never recorded, including "Indian Cowboy," his long-ago circus song.

He also finished a long-in-the-borning semiautobiographical novel called *Super Reverb*. Over the years he has busied himself producing other artists, including Jimmie Dale Gilmore's and Butch Hancock's first albums (as well as Jimmie's most recent, *Come On Back*), and the first two "new" Flatlanders studio albums. He has also toured on and off with a songwriters' circle that has included Lyle Lovett, John Hiatt, and Guy Clark.

In 1998, he was part of the *Los Super Seven* debut album, alongside Tex-Mex music legends Freddy Fender, Flaco Jimenez, and Ruben Ramos, along with Doug Sahm, Rick Treviño, and David Hidalgo and Cesar Rosas of Los Lobos. He shared the album's Grammy Award for Best Mexican-American/Tejano Music Performance.

Seven years later, he returned for Los Super Seven's third album, *Heard It on the X*, which also featured Ramos, Treviño, Clarence "Gatemouth" Brown, Lyle Lovett, Delbert McClinton, and the Mavericks' Raul Malo. Ely killed with a propulsive, horn-driven version of fellow West Texan Bobby Fuller's "Let Her Dance."

As if all that were not enough, there was, of course, the re-emergence of the Flatlanders in 2002. A decade-and-change later, they are still going strong.

Along the way, he evolved into one of the elder statesmen of what had come to be called Americana music, although Ely treated that genre-labeling with the same out-of-pocket disdain with which he had always regarded all the arbitrary classifications of his music. Once you define it, his thinking went, you destroy it.

In spite of that, or perhaps because of it, he became an unofficial mentor and inspiration to younger performers. My own subjective list of Ely protégés might include Robert Earl Keen, Ryan Bingham, the Dixie Chicks, Todd Snider, Patricia Vonne, Steve Earle, Rosie Flores, Lyle Lovett, and more.

I didn't take on the world for fortune or fame
I set my direction with a flickering flame
Oh, mama, forget about the past
It's been a long time coming
Satisfied at last

"Satisfied at Last"
JOE ELY

———

Satisfied at Last, on Rack 'Em, is his latest album as of this writing. Though the title may suggest complacency, there is little doubt that the restless spirit that has driven Ely his entire life is still behind the wheel. But at the same time, there is an awareness of shrinking horizons and a certain sense of finite time. The most affecting track on the record is, to my mind, not one of Ely's own, but his cover of Billy Joe Shaver's triumphant and tender valedictory, "Live Forever."

"[The album is] a bit about mortality," he admitted. "We ain't getting any younger, and you've got to look that in the eye."

"Those records in the '80s with the loud rock and roll band felt right at the time," Ely says on his website bio. "They were boisterous and rowdy, and that's the way I felt then. This record really sums up where I am right now."

That younger man, gunslinging his way through the Saturday night honky-tonks, never seemed satisfied in the least. But the 2014 Joe Ely who regards that younger man with bemused affection knows that satisfied doesn't mean settling for less. It means being at peace with the path you've taken and the choices you've made.

"It wouldn't be right for me to sing about raising hell and shooting holes in the ceiling," he said. "That's just not where I'm at right now. But I am having probably as good or better a time making music than I've ever had in my life. I work in the studio all the time, and I find *that* real satisfying.

"When you're setting out in life, you really project things the way you think they're gonna be when you're sixty. But really, every single thing that I did, I never expected any of the things that happened to me, good or bad."

River's on the rise
Crows are in the skies
Look at that big yella cornbread moon
Now you're lookin'
You feel somethin' cookin'

"Cornbread Moon"
JOE ELY

———

He's out there tonight, somewhere, I once wrote about Joe Ely.

Maybe he's in a coffee shop, mulling over the news of the day and jotting down a scrap of lyric on the torn corner of a paper placemat. Maybe it's after last call, and he's circling a pool table somewhere in some downtown, looking for the perfect three-ball combo.

Perhaps he's tuning his guitar backstage before tonight's show, eyeing the dressing room deli tray and wishing he had a cigarette. Outside the door, past the stage, he can hear the murmur of the audience and, perhaps he is reminded of the soft rumble of surf on the long-ago Venice beach, at the edge of an ocean he could not have imagined as a child.

He might be sitting in a hotel room late at night, vaguely pissed off and lonesome, missing his wife and daughter and decent Mexican food. Wondering why he ever got into this racket. There's a rerun of *M*A*S*H* on the television, if he cares to watch. He doesn't. Restless, wanting to be somewhere else, the night over and done with, this city—what city is it again?—behind him.

It could be he's rolling down the road at ten past three in the morning, fast asleep in the belly of the tour bus, just another iron monster on the Interstate, rumbling past the exit ramps and the small, dark towns dreaming their small, dark dreams. He's dreaming too . . .

Maybe he's a little drunk on top-shelf wine somewhere, although he doesn't really drink that much. He's laughing with friends and old compadres, making up new lies and making all the old lies sound true. Someone pulls out a guitar and says, "Hey, check this out . . ." He'll be hungover in the morning, but the morning is very far away . . .

He's out there. Tonight. Just like he always dreamed of being. "I never set out to go and do anything on a grand scale," he said. "I just happened to be able to go from city to city and play shows. There's a kind of fulfillment in just being able to stay on the road and play music every night."

He's out there . . .

* * *

Outward, upward, off and away! Anywhere but here!
Anytime but now! Anything but this!

JIMMIE DALE GILMORE'S
favorite call to arms

———

Jimmie Gilmore reentered the world of music just as a new year was dawning. He left Denver and Maharaji's ashram and arrived back in Austin on New Year's Eve 1980 and performed that very night, the last night at the Armadillo before it closed, as a sing-along guest, completing yet another circle in the

Flatlanders' saga (Gilmore's Hub City Movers had played the joint's opening night in 1970).

He began to play some of the same acoustic rooms that Butch frequented—the Alamo Lounge, emmajoe's, and the Cactus Café. He fell in with a younger singer/songwriter community, many of whom would go on to bigger things. Gilmore shared many a bill with the likes of Nanci Griffith, Lyle Lovett, and Lucinda Williams, all of them playing for tips and a small but growing fan base.

It was at the Alamo Lounge that he met his third wife, Janet Branch. A pretty brunette who was working on a 1981 campaign for the liberal agriculture commissioner Jim Hightower, Branch and her coworkers stopped in for beer one night when Jimmie and Butch were playing. After Hightower had his ass handed to him in the election by Texas governor Rick Perry, Branch needed a job. She began to waitress at some of the same joints Gilmore played. Propinquity begat romance. The pair married in 1986.

"I fell in love with his voice first," she recalled. "I think it was some kind of past life thing. We went out a few times, but didn't really get together until about a year and a half later."

For a time, the couple lived in the building that Joe Ely was converting into a recording studio adjacent to his own home. Ely had produced an independent single for Gilmore, a delightfully rocking number called "She's All Grown Up (But She Still Likes to Rock 'n' Roll)." It was Gilmore's first time in front of a studio mike since the Flatlanders had gone to Nashville.

At roughly the same time, Gilmore had caught the eye of a manager named Mike Crowley, who told him, "If you ever want to go for a career, let me know."

As Ely recounted to *Dirty Linen*, "Jimmie lived out here in the country next to me, where I now have my studio and we put a few songs down on tape." Ely was signed to the Hightone label at the time and had entrée to the label's A&R guys ("A&R" stands for "Artists and Repertoire"; basically they are talent scouts).

Ely continued, "The Hightone guys came down one time and I slipped the tape into my machine, saying, 'If you want to hear something, listen to this guy.' They immediately perked up their ears."

Gilmore released his first solo album, *Fair & Square*, on the Hightone label in 1988. He was forty-three years old.

Ely produced the record, which was recorded in part at his own studio. He told the magazine, "That was nice for me, in that I'd wanted to have something released by Jimmie for so long. You can only keep those songs you hear in person in your head for so long, and you want to share it with others."

Fair & Square is a good template for what would become Gilmore's solo career: there's a Townes Van Zandt cover, songs by Ely and Hancock, a yodeling, buoyant version of the Marty Robbins hit "Singing the Blues," and a pair of songs by Gilmore's guitarist at the time, a terrific young songwriter named David Halley.

One of Butch's songs on the album, "Just a Wave," is a lilting, languid breakup song with one of the great kiss-off lines of all time: "Babe, you're just a wave / You're not the water." By contrast, a reprise of Gilmore's "All Grown Up" sounds like it could have been lifted from the rockingest chapter of Buddy Holly's playbook. For the balance of the album, the honkytonk seems to take precedence over the coffeehouse.

People magazine said of the effort, "This record grows on you, true. But only after it sounds terrific in the first place." *USA Today* named it one of the five top country albums of the year. The Austin release party for *Fair & Square* also marked the debut of Gilmore's long-running Wednesday night residency at the original Threadgill's restaurant, which became an appointment event for Austin music fans for years.

Was the finished product folk, rock, country, or some sort of uniquely West Texas musical fusion? The correct answer is "yes."

Jimmie Dale Gilmore, also on Hightone, followed a year later. Recorded in Nashville with Music City sidemen, and produced by Bruce Bromberg and fellow Lubbockite Lloyd Maines, the album avoided the dreaded sophomore slump while showcasing more of Gilmore's original material. Including two cowrites with Butch, Gilmore penned half the songs on the album, including a remake of "Dallas" that was a loping country two-step, a vast departure from Joe Ely's jet-fueled rocker of the same song. A bouncy take on the Webb Pierce hit "Honky-Tonk Song" and a reeling dance hall cover of Boz Scaggs's "Up to You" helped flesh out the package. Despite the Nashville pedigree, *Jimmie Dale Gilmore* was never attractive to mainstream country radio. Too much old-school twang and two-step melodies for besotted Garth Brooks fans.

But the album wasn't all honky-tonk. The Gilmore/Hancock composition "See the Way" was a stately call to self-awareness ("You'll find some healers and some forgivers / Deep in the heart of eternity") very much in keeping with Gilmore's spiritual quests.

Janet and Jimmie had married in 1986, and as time went on she eventually grew to match and even surpass his ardor for Buddhism and its teachings.

"Janet and I came to Buddhism by different tracks," he said, adding that their shared devotion might have saved their marriage.

"Janet started studying with a different teacher, and a few years ago he ordained her as the teacher for our little group [which also often includes Hancock and Ely]. He picked the right person. She's the one who has the most understanding and the most knowledge. We have book learning, but she has that, and a gut-level understanding, too. Like she was born with it."

By the mid-1990s, Gilmore gradually came to feel disconnected from Maharaji and some of the Vedantic teachings. "By this time, I knew enough about the Vedanta to understand a critique of it. And I agreed with the critique. Buddhism was an entirely different thing—nontheistic, though not necessarily atheistic. That blew my mind. Nothing to do with an external higher power. It all has to do with awareness and mindfulness."

Nineteen ninety-one's *After Awhile* saw Gilmore make a move from Hightone to the bigger Elektra label (via its boutique Elektra/Nonesuch imprint), and began to recast him as less a honky-tonk singer than a singer/songwriter who happened to lean toward country.

Produced by Stephen Bruton (Bonnie Raitt, Kris Kristofferson), *After Awhile* was Gilmore's most self-contained effort to date. He wrote or cowrote all but one of the album's twelve songs (the ringer being a Butch song, naturally). Gilmore used the occasion to revisit some of his earliest Flatlanders-era tunes, such as "Tonight I Think I'm Gonna Go Downtown" and "Number 16." *Rolling Stone* called the album "the work of a great American songwriter."

But the album is more noteworthy for what it represents. *After Awhile* marked the beginning of Gilmore's most sustained period of commercial and critical ascent.

The three albums he released in seven years, *Spinning Around the Sun* (1993), *Braver Newer World* (1996), and *One Endless Night* (2000), earned the kinds of kudos and honors that most artists only dream of. He was named Country Artist of the Year three times by *Rolling Stone*. *Salon* magazine called him a "Zen country singer" in one rave. The *New York Times Magazine* said, "He has acquired a large, devoted following who buy his records the way the readers of, say, Dan DeLillo or Louise Erdrich buy the next book: because there's one out there."

Spinning Around the Sun, with its mix of ethereal and timeless originals ("Where You Going" and "Another Colorado") and nervy covers (Elvis's "I Was the One" and Hank's "I'm So Lonesome I Could Cry"), was nominated for a Grammy for Best Contemporary Folk Album. It was the first of three eventual Grammy nominations, a hat trick none of his fellow Flatlanders have ever come close to managing.

Of that album, the *Village Voice*'s preeminent music critic Robert Christgau wrote, "I doubt I'll hear a more gorgeous country record—maybe a more gorgeous record—anytime soon."

The T-Bone Burnet–produced *Braver Newer World* earned a second Grammy nomination for Gilmore, but he lost to Bruce Springsteen's melancholy *The Ghost of Tom Joad*. "Jimmie didn't make it," someone said afterward. "But he was in pretty good company." *Rolling Stone* wrote, "His preferred subject is contemplation, the tension of decision as you stand at the crossroads."

He appeared on Jay Leno's *Tonight Show*, dueting on "Dallas" with Natalie Merchant, and appeared in a fashion layout in *Esquire*. One night he was in a bookstore in Austin and spotted five major magazines on the shelf, and he realized he was featured in each one.

Some of the best accolades are the ones you never see coming. On the road one night, he found himself circling above—yes!—the Dallas–Fort Worth airport. As he told the *New York Times*, no one recognized him, but the front half of the plane burst into a spontaneous sing-along of "Dallas." "It took every ounce of self-restraint I had not to yell, 'I wrote that song!'"

He also managed to achieve a minor slice of immortality when he landed a cameo as Smokey, the nervous bowler who ends up on the wrong end of John Goodman's .45 pistol in the

1998 Coen brothers' cult classic, *The Big Lebowski*. "Mark it an eight, Dude" may be as famous a Jimmie Dale Gilmore line as any he ever sang. Possibly to his chagrin.

He has never had a breakout hit (the Hank Williams cover was supposed to accomplish that), but he never shared the same animus toward Nashville that some Texas musicians use as a crutch. He made three records there, after all. "I really don't believe in those geographical, artificial categorizations," he said. "The music is the music, you know?"

True to that ethos, he has branched off on esoteric projects as it suits him. In 1994, the Sub Pop label released an EP featuring Gilmore swapping songs (including a Townes cover and his own "Tonight I Think I'm Gonna Go Downtown") with Seattle grunge rockers Mudhoney.

More recently, in 2011, he recorded *Heirloom Music*, an album of bluegrass/acoustic/traditional music, with the Wronglers, a group of part-time Bay Area musicians affiliated with San Francisco's Hardly Strictly Bluegrass Festival. It didn't hurt that the Wronglers were founded by the late billionaire philanthropist and financier Warren Hellman, who also underwrote the festival.

The projects are reminiscent of the Flatlanders in their way, said Gilmore. "My deal with them is based on friendship versus hired guns. They [the two band collaborations] both arose spontaneously, from our shared love of certain kinds of music and the friendship that we all have between us."

Gilmore nailed his third Grammy nomination with his most recent solo project, another album of "old-timey" music, 2005's *Come On Back* (on Rounder Records).

Once more produced by Ely, it closes yet another circle for Gilmore. It is an album chock-full of country and honky-tonk classics from Ernest Tubb, Hank Snow, Marty Robbins, Johnny Cash, the Carter Family, and more, and it is dedicated to the memory of his father, Brian Gilmore. On the inside cover is a photo of the guitar Earl Scruggs encouraged Jimmie to buy so very long ago, and a photo of Brian's vintage Fender electric, too.

He's also passed along what he's learned. "Since I've been teaching songwriting at the Omega Institute [for the past eighteen years], I think I've learned probably more than my students have," he said. The class, held at the nonprofit center for holistic studies in Rhinebeck, New York, is an annual endeavor close to his heart.

"Teaching forced me to articulate my ideas about songwriting and I think that between teaching and thinking so much about the music that my dad and I loved, I had a renewed appreciation for these unpretentious songs (on *Come On Back*). They're short, to the point, economical, like folk art, really. Joe kept saying, 'We just gotta stay out of the way of these songs,' and I think he was right."

The circle closes, but the search goes on; the circle and the search are the same, after all. "Everything that is, is a product of the interplay of everything that is," he said, sounding certain and seeking, both at once. "None of it exists on its own."

One day in 2012 the Flatlanders were sitting for a radio interview, and Jimmie was talking about the evolution that has formed the template for his life and music.

"In my own perception," he was saying, "I've changed a lot in that time (since the Flatlanders' first iteration). I used to think that I was the best singer in the band. And I realized I wasn't. In lots of ways, my whole life has been that way. I used to think I was a lot more cosmic and ethereal and perfect than it turned out I really was. I haven't even gotten very good at humility."

Butch Hancock wasn't going to pass up the chance to gig his boyhood friend. Especially on the radio.

"With me it was just the opposite," he said dryly. "I started out really humble, and now I realize finally that I know everything that's needed to know. I just don't tell very much of it."

And Jimmie Dale Gilmore, the once-and-future Flatlander, just laughed.

* * *

Muddy water in the Rio Grande
Fast eddies and slow quicksand
A gypsy moth and some dragonflies
I love the way you roll your eyes

"Barefoot Prints"
BUTCH HANCOCK

———

Go to Butch Hancock's still-a-work-in-progress house today out in the vastness of the Big Bend desert in far West Texas, and you will find a mosaic of techniques—adobe here, straw-bale construction there, beer can walls over yonder, and a bevy of old Airstream trailers scattered around like placid, grazing metallic cattle. All over the map, just like its owner.

If Joe pursued the most conventional pop music career path—get a record contract, get a manager, record, tour, re-peat and Jimmie eventually racked up three Grammy nomina-tions and a major-label contract or two of his own—that left Butch to follow the most iconoclastic path of the trio, one that anticipated the current DIY boom by a couple of decades or so.

His first album, 1978's *West Texas Waltzes and Dust Blown Tractor Tunes*, was released on his own Rainlight imprint. Though the term "boutique label" was yet years off, that's es-sentially what Rainlight was—an autonomous entity that let Hancock record his music, his way. In spirit if not in sound, the label was true to the punk rock spit-and-baling-wire work ethic.

Produced by Hancock and Ely (credited as "Earl Epiphone") and recorded at Ely's farmhouse outside of Lubbock, the album featured Butch on "voice, guitar, foot, and harmonica." Period.

Black-and-white photos of a prairie windmill and what looks like some sort of pumping station, along with Butch's hand-lettered titles, completed the LP package. As Ely recalled, "We pretty much just turned on the machine and made a record in two days."

The tracks were deliberately spare arrangements that harkened back to early Dylan and Woody Guthrie (and even earlier Lomax-era folk and blues field recordings), both in sound and in the populist tone of tunes like "Dryland Farm," "They Say It's a Good Land," "Little Coyote Waltz," and "I Grew to Be a Stranger." Best of all, though, is the sly, funny, sexy "West Texas Waltz," which Emmylou Harris also cut and which remains a staple in the Flatlanders' set to this day. Teasing about something so delicious that it can hardly be spoken of out loud, and featuring some of his most buoyant rhyming, Hancock makes us wish we were all in on the secret:

> Only two things are better than milkshakes and malts
> And one's dancin' like the dickens to the West Texas waltz
> And the other is something that really is nothing
> To speak of, it's something to do
> But if you've done it before, you'll be doing it some more
> As soon as the dancin' is through

"Townes Van Zandt said to me one time, 'All you West Texas guys have that High Plains air in your sound,'" Hancock told Christopher Oglesby. "'I can't tell whether it's in your voices or in the general feel of your music. But there is something about that West Texas wind in all your songs.'"

That observation was never more evident than on Butch's first album. The spare production and Hancock's sand-scrubbed vocals were reflections of the hardscrabble landscape. Music and topography—one moving, the other immobile.

Transitory, yet fixed; that's appropriately West Texas, according to Hancock:

"Nothing looks like it belongs there because, in fact, it doesn't. Everything out there is imported. Most of the dirt blew in from the next state. Literally, everything out there is an applied object.

"The great thing about West Texas," he added, "is that any idea or stimulation you have out there, you have the opportunity to ponder it awhile. You see something on the horizon thirty miles ahead when you're driving down the highway and it's going to be in your consciousness for at least the next thirty minutes while you get there."

Or, as he put it another time, "There's knowledge in the wind. As it blows down the plains, all the way from Canada, it's just holding its own. And then, all of a sudden, it hits Palo Duro Canyon near Amarillo and Yellow House Canyon, outside of Lubbock, and those two jolts shake a lot of shit out of there."

If *West Texas Waltzes and Dust Blown Tractor Tunes* was Hancock's equivalent to *The Freewheelin' Bob Dylan*, then its follow-up, 1979's *The Wind's Dominion*, was his *Blonde on Blonde*.

Recorded in Lubbock's Caldwell Studios and produced by Butch and the ubiquitous Lloyd Maines, the album was a sprawling two-disc set utilizing a full band (including Joe and Jimmie on vocals) for a sweeping, cinematic effect.

The material matched the production, and featured songwriting that was, while not necessarily better, far more wide-ranging than that on Hancock's debut.

The songs, especially "Mario y Maria," "Smokin' in the Rain," "The Gift Horse of Mercy," and "Capture, Fracture and the Rapture," resound with allusions and surreal scenarios that bump together like boxcars in a switching yard.

The initial impression is a cascade of images and characters that stampede like the herd of mustangs galloping across the album's cover. The secondary impression is "too much," case in point being the curious a cappella opener "Sea's Deadog Catch" (credited to "Milo Flagg," whoever that might be) and the mournful waltz "Eternal Triangles," both of which seem like filler, especially against masterful vignettes like "Row of Dominoes" and "Personal Rendition of the Blues."

The showpiece in an album full of showpieces may be the ten-minute country-rocker "Only Born," which is his own Dylan-esque "Sad-Eyed Lady of the Lowlands," with the same push/pull romantic tension ("She's givin' him the old take or leave it / And he's sure takin' it hard / 'Cause he ain't her lover anymore / He's just her bodyguard").

Hancock would release seven albums in nine years up through 1986, including a live set, *Firewater Seeks Its Own Level*, recorded at the Alamo Lounge in Austin, and *Yella Rose*, which features duets with Louisiana singer Marce Lacouture.

Fools fall in love
Wise men may fall, too
But a wise man hits the bottom
While a fool just falls on through

"Fools Fall in Love"
BUTCH HANCOCK

———

Hancock moved to Austin in 1976 and quickly took up residency at beer joints like the Split Rail and the Austin Outhouse and listening rooms like the Alamo Lounge and, later, emmajoe's.

What he didn't do is advance his career (if indeed he even bothered to view his artistic life through that prism) in any symmetrical, conventional way.

Ely's acclaimed first album featured four of Butch's songs, Hancock's first proxy exposure outside of Lubbock or Austin. Jerry Jeff Walker, the Texas Tornados, and, as mentioned,

Emmylou Harris would also go on to record Hancock covers. The Texas Senate passed a resolution in 1977 commending his photography, art, architecture, and music, and noting, "he was and is one of the best tractor drivers in all of the Texas Panhandle."

But of major label deals, booking agents, organized tours behind new album releases, press agents, and all the other infrastructure that goes with a professional music career, there were few signs. *Texas Monthly* magazine called him "the best-known unknown on the folk circuit."

It was probably just as well. Not only were many of Hancock's songs too lyrically dense and musically unclassifiable to be easily marketable, but he keeps more irons in the fire than a blacksmith on Benzedrine. Focusing on a linear path to pop culture celebrity would mean less time for songwriting, photography, art, video, architecture, river rafting, and all the other mutually reinforcing endeavors that provide Hancock with a renewable reservoir of creativity.

Lack of a work ethic has never been his problem. "There's incredible relaxation with staying busy with so many different things. A lot of my work is a form of play," he said to *Texas Monthly* in 1991.

"I've never really pursued a major label," he told the *Texas Monthly* writer. "Why do I want to sell more records? It's the old Groucho deal of not wanting to be in any group that would have me. So I'm gonna go on doing what I'm gonna do, and if people pick up on it, that's wonderful. And if they don't, I can always drive a tractor."

"The fame seems to be the least comfortable aspect of his musicianship," said his wife, Adrienne Evans-Stark. "He doesn't mind that people know who he is; it's just that for a lot of people, the fame is what they're seeking. At some point he realized that that doesn't fill your cup."

Evans-Stark first experienced Hancock as a fan, way back

in the Alamo Lounge days. She and Hancock dated for a while, but eventually she moved to Santa Fe, where she married and had two daughters. But she hastened to add, "We kept our friendship. We were always really good as friends."

In 1996 the pair reunited, and they soon had a son, Rory.

He would eventually attract label attention, of a sort. The Sugar Hill label, best known for its bluegrass and roots music catalog, would put out two compilations of Butch's Rainlight output in 1989 and 1993 (*Own and Own* and *Own the Way Over Here*, respectively). The label would also release an album of new Hancock material, *Eats Away the Night*, in 1995.

That album, produced by guitarist and songwriter Gurf Morlix, who also produced Lucinda Williams, Ray Wylie Hubbard, Robert Earl Keen, and Tom Russell, was a full-blown effort, featuring the rhythm section from Lucinda's band, along with Joe Ely Band alumni Jesse Taylor and Ponty Bone.

It also featured a bevy of fresh new songs, the standouts of which included the bluesy, gently rocking love song "Moanin' of the Midnight Train" and the sardonic "Welcome to the Real World Kid," along with the hiccupping, Buddy Holly–like word rush of "Baby Be Mine" ("I ain't a-gonna let nobody humble me / I ain't a-gonna bumble like a bumble bee / I ain't a-gonna stumble and I ain't a-gonna step out of line / So don't gimme no maybe, baby, baby, baby be mine").

Reviewing the album for Amazon.com, *Washington Post* music critic Geoffrey Himes observed, "This is the first Hancock album to be thoughtfully conceived, carefully recorded with a rehearsed band and efficiently distributed, and the results throw the best possible light on Hancock's raucous sense of humor and his passionate embrace of the world's most farfetched possibilities. . . .

"The producer and players add rhythmic muscle and harmonic flesh to Hancock's songs without ever getting in the way of the words, which are the main attraction. . . . Four of his older songs ('If You Were a Bluebird,' 'Boxcars,' 'One Kiss' and 'Baby Be Mine') finally receive worthy arrangements."

From his home base in Austin, Hancock lined up acoustic tours of Europe and the U.K. He even toured Russia as part of a goodwill group of Texas musicians in 1987.

Back in the Lone Star State the following year, he helped create and coproduce a syndicated live music cable television show, *Dixie's Bar and Bus Stop*, which captured almost one hundred performances by Jerry Jeff Walker, Terry Allen, Tommy Hancock's Supernatural Family Band, and others.

Nineteen ninety was a year of teeming activity even by Hancock's multitasking standards. He opened an art gallery and performance space in an old Studebaker dealership in downtown Austin and dubbed it Lubbock or Leave It. (Oh, for the days of cheap Austin real estate!)

The place was basically a look inside Butch's brain. He had his photography studio and cassette-duplicating setup in the back. Out front were a stage and a revolving series of exhibits, including Hancock's photography and Australian aboriginal art. A little retail setup sold everything from Supernatural Family Band tapes to Townes Van Zandt songbooks to handmade jewelry to Stubb's Bar-B-Q Sauce.

Michael Ventura came and read poetry, Jo Harvey Allen (Terry's playwright wife) staged scenes, and, on one particularly memorable evening, Sharon Ely curated a "Black Velvet Fashion Show" inspired by cheap motel paintings of Elvis and big-eyed Indian kids. The Flatlanders performed, with Butch, Jimmie, and Joe sporting outlandish *Cat in the Hat*–style velvet patchwork stovepipe hats.

(The place closed in 1996, when Butch chose a radical, but totally predictably unpredictable Hancockian change of scenery and relocated to . . . well, you'll see.)

Then there was *No 2 Alike*, his marathon six-night stand at the Cactus Café from January 30 through February 4—140 original songs, no repeats. The Flatlanders (all of them, with Steve Wesson and Tony Pearson) played that one, too, their first "official" reunion in almost a decade. Tickets were five dollars a night, fifteen dollars for the whole shebang.

It was a marathon for fans and performers alike. Critic Peter Blackstock, summoning up the bop-till-you-drop rush of the event for the *Austin American-Statesman*, wrote afterwards, "It was billed as *No 2 Alike*, but it threatened to leave no two alive. . . . Playing a total of 140 original songs wasn't enough for Hancock. Coordinating a crew of more than two-dozen special guests wasn't enough. Setting a new attendance record for the Cactus wasn't enough.

"Closing the event with a 27-minute song ('Last Long Silver Dollar') was, finally, enough."

Hancock recorded the entire thing and created a *No 2 Alike* tape club, wherein subscribers could sign up for a series of fourteen cassettes documenting all six nights.

At the same time Lubbock or Leave It was operating, he toured around the country, recorded, did a thirty-day tour of Austin venues to promote the development of public murals around the city, and contributed songs and music to, and acted in, *Chippy*, a stage production by Terry and Jo Harvey Allen about a Depression-era hooker in the West Texas oil patch.

The things we go through to go through the things we go through.

BUTCH HANCOCK

———

And then he gave it all up, moved to the desert, and became Lawrence of frickin' Arabia.

Wait, that's not quite it.

For several years, Hancock had been hooking up with a group called Far Flung Adventures, an outfitter near Big Bend National Park that guided rafters through the canyons of the elbow-shaped stretch of the Rio Grande that separated Texas from the Mexican states of Chihuahua and Coahuila. The guides would paddle all day and Butch would serenade the paying customers around the campfire at night; talk about "unplugged." Mariscal, Boquillas, and Santa Elena Canyons are as isolated as it is possible to be and still nominally be on U.S. soil.

Over time, Butch graduated to camp cook and then, after some training, to river guide. Singing goddam boatman, just like in Venice.

Except Big Bend was nothing at all like Venice. It was like Mars.

For people accustomed to greener, wetter landscapes, it's hard to convey how utterly alien the Big Bend country can seem (technically, the region is called the Trans-Pecos and is part of the northern Chihuahuan desert). Mountain ranges such as the Chisos and the Sierra del Carmen bolt up without preamble out of the desert floor, and the border river winds hidden between walls of stone 1,200 feet high. Everything, as the saying goes, either stabs, stings, or bites.

An old vaquero once described the region as being a place "where the rainbows wait for the rain, and the big river is kept in a stone box, and water runs uphill and mountains float in the air, except at night when they go away to play with other mountains."

In the fall of 1996, after folding Lubbock or Leave It, Butch unplugged his Airstream trailer from its South Austin trailer park home and carted it down to an old ghost town west of the park called Terlingua.

Just a few crumbling adobes and stacked-rock houses, a restaurant/bar called the Starlight Theater, owing to its onetime-caved-in roof, and a general store with an expansive front portal perfect for twilight beer-sipping and bullshitting, Terlingua had enjoyed a brief heyday during which cinnabar (from which mercury is derived) was heavily mined. But the mines played out, as mines will do, and Terlingua began a long slide into irrelevance, until it was rediscovered by chili cooks, river boatmen, a few hardy artists, a smattering of ex-cowboys, a couple of professional misanthropes, and other off-the-grid types.

As Joe Ely is fond of saying, to get to Butch's front door, you drive west until you can't stand it anymore and then go south for two hours.

It was three hundred miles to the nearest airport. You could throw a rock and hit Mexico. A flat tire could be a life-or-death dilemma. It suited Hancock just fine.

"It all has to do with simplification," he said, a year or so after the move. "Trying to home in on the 'is-ness' of everything, just that extended moment. In Austin, that was always my thing too, but it was time for a change of pace. Robert Johnson said you gots to keep movin', and I hadn't been moving enough lately."

Needless to say, he wasn't going to join the other old farts on the Terlingua Trading Company porch, drinking beer and watching the sunset reflected off the distant Chisos Mountains.

Before 1997 was done, he had a new album of original material ready for release on Rainlight. Most of the songs on the Butch 'n' Joe–produced *You Coulda Walked Around the World* were written with a desert horizon outside the window, and songs like "Barefoot Prints," "Red Blood (Drippin' from the Moon)," and "Hidin' in the Hills" all evoke a sense of remoteness and space. The loveliest song on the album, "Roll Around," was actually written for *Chippy*, but even it has some

Trans-Pecos mysticism in its bones: "Ancient mountains . . . Chills and fevers / Empty roads and fields of flowers / Dusty beds . . . hangin' gardens / The golden light's still in my eyes, love."

Adrienne, an acupuncturist and EMT, joined him full-time in 1998 and spent a decade in the desert. In that time, she agitated against the proposed border wall near Presidio, lobbied for the establishment of a mobile mammogram service for the region (the nearest breast cancer treatment facility was in Odessa, a five-hundred-mile round-trip from Terlingua), and trained as a tracker for lost Big Bend tourists (a two-year-old was her biggest save).

She credited Butch with making those things and her other volunteer work possible. "He's there like a rock," she said. "I was able to accomplish these things because of having such a solid person in my life. If I didn't have him, I couldn't have done any of these things for my community."

Right now, she and Butch ping-pong between the Big Bend and their home in Wimberley, just outside of Austin. But as soon as their son finishes high school, she said, she's Terlingua-bound.

In the meantime, he has a new album, the first since 2006's politically charged *War and Peace*. ("He has been paying attention," said the reviewer in *No Depression*. "And, man, is he pissed. . . . it's a seething, blistering rage unleashed, personal and macro, against the forces of No Dang Good.")

The new disc, *Seven Cities of Gold*, is an eleven-song cycle, some of whose tunes date back as far as 1979, while others are freshly minted.

"It's kind of like a Flatlanders album with me singing 'em all," Hancock said. "Jimmie and Joe are on two or three of them, and the very last song, it goes out with Jimmie singing one chorus, and Joe singing the other.

"It's not as topical as *War and Peace*, exactly; just a different slice of life."

For that aforementioned last song, "No Thing," Hancock borrowed a verse from the 1,100-year-old *Diamond Sutra* to hang his hook on:

Thus shall you think of all this fleeting world
Of star at dawn, of bubbles in a stream
A flash of lighting in a summer cloud
A flickering glance at a phantom in a dream

Of course, he couldn't leave it alone. "I changed the first line to fit more into a song set in Texas and the Western World: 'Think about it, darlin'.' Then it flows beautifully!"

Driving that tractor ten hours a day so long ago might have seemed like unbearable tedium to anyone without Butch Hancock's well-tuned perspective. For him it was liberation.

"Sitting up on the tractor, watching each little clod made up of grains of sand getting turned by the plow and becoming a row of dirt a mile long, suddenly you are into the scope of the universe," he told Christopher Oglesby. "The whole scale of everything is right there . . . the universe in a grain of sand."

PART FIVE   *The Return*

A lot of bands pretend to be friends; these were
friends who once pretended to be a band.

DON MCLEESE
in *No Depression*

CHAPTER 11

More a Band

They didn't disappear when the Flatlanders dissipated, of course, any more than a freight train evaporates when it at last passes over the distant horizon.

Butch, Jimmie, and Joe had been friends before there was such a thing as the Flatlanders, and friends they were still.

They hung out together, especially after the three of them eventually relocated to Austin (Jimmie and Joe are still here; Butch commutes periodically from Terlingua). They sang each other's songs; played, produced, and swapped vocals on each other's records; showed up at each other's gigs; performed in various configurations—Butch and Jimmie toured Australia together in 1990 and released a live album, *Two Roads*, on Virgin Records. From their perspective, nothing much had changed.

The Flatlanders, over whom so much fuss was made by outsiders, were never the be-all and end-all of Hancock's, Ely's, and Gilmore's careers; the band was just one boxcar on their freight train.

"People used to think it was this crushing blow," said Gilmore of the Nashville album's nonrelease. "But it wasn't, because the whole thing had come together by accident. So it wasn't like this great life plan had fallen apart. It was a disappointment, but it wasn't shattering. We were still the same people."

But their fans did not move on. Quite the opposite. Though only a relative handful of people in Lubbock, Austin, and Kerrville ever got to see the Flatlanders play, a mystique grew up around the group. Hancock, Ely, and Gilmore talked about the Flatlanders in interviews, and as their celebrity expanded, so did the buzz about these Nashville recordings no one had ever heard. To fans, the Flatlanders' songs were the Rosetta Stone of West Texas music.

To make it even more tantalizing, the three would occasionally find themselves onstage together, once in a while even on purpose. There was an "official" reunion at the Kerrville Folk Festival in 1977, at least one show at the Cactus Café in Austin, a miniset during Butch Hancock's *No 2 Alike* marathon, and other occasions as serendipity permitted. When Jimmie and Janet Gilmore got married at Joe and Sharon's place, the trio ended up on a flatbed truck singing as soon as the vows concluded. Tony Pearson says they even played his dad's eightieth birthday party in 2002. And there was a blink-and-you'll-miss-'em set at the Broken Spoke honky-tonk during one year's South by Southwest music festival. But that's getting ahead of the story.

In either 1980 or January of 1981, eight or so years after they were recorded, the Flatlanders' Nashville tracks were released on LP, not in the United States but in England, on the Charly record label, which John Singleton said was a foreign affiliate of Sun Entertainment Corporation.

The Charly release almost certainly hinged on Ely's growing popularity in the U.K. This was about the time when Ely was touring England with the Clash on their *London Calling* dates. Having the imprimatur of the hottest band in England didn't hurt Ely's status among his British fans a bit.

Entitled *One Road More*, the album was a simple sepia-and-white package featuring a grainy blown-up photo (staged by Hancock) of the five guys leaning up against a plank wall. There's Tony (with mandolin), Steve (with a feather in his cowboy hat and looking a great deal like the poet Richard Brautigan), Jimmie (crouching down and hugging a pooch who may have been Sharon Ely's dog), Joe (in profile, boot cocked against the wall, with a moustache), and Butch, arms crossed, looking like one of the Earp brothers in an Old West tintype.

The album contained seventeen tracks, apparently the sum total of the band's recordings for Shelby Singleton.

This was not the only overseas release of the Flatlanders tracks. The Spanish label Zafiro licensed the music and the artwork and released its version of *One Road More* in 1989.

Two Flatlanders songs, "Dallas" and "Tonight I Think I'm Gonna Go Downtown," also appeared on a Charly compilation, *T for Texas*, which was released in advance of *One Road More* in 1979.

Ten years later, the long arc of the Flatlanders bent a little bit more when Rounder Records released a domestic CD, the aptly titled *More a Legend Than A Band*, which contained thirteen of the seventeen Nashville tracks (minus the covers "Waitin' for a Train" and "Hello Stranger," Jimmie's "Not So Long Ago," and Al Strehli's "I Know You").

(Rounder's Bill Nowlin wrote me in an e-mail, "The contract was signed on April 1, 1989, between Rounder and Sun Entertainment—for an advance of $1,000. John Singleton signed on behalf of Sun. . . . the album was released in January 1990.")

The cover, featuring another image from the same photo shoot that yielded the Charly cover, put the guys adrift on a prairie, the vast void of blue sky behind them, looking like so many cowboy-hatted Easter Island statues. They look at once both vulnerable and cohesive, a duality that finds its parallel in the music.

To American fans, the release of *More A Legend Than A Band* was nothing short of a revelation. Ely, Gilmore, and Hancock had been singing each other's songs for years, but here were the original performances, intact.

(In 1995, perhaps coincident with Gilmore's rise as a solo artist and his Grammy nomination, Sun Records re-re-released the Nashville tracks as "Unplugged," by "Jimmie Dale Gilmore and the Flatlanders, including Joe Ely and Butch Hancock.")

"Every genre has its Ur-band," wrote *Esquire* in 2009, "those lesser-known dudes who create the sound that goes mainstream without them. . . . alt-country has the Flatlanders."

To aficionados of the roots-centric, singer/songwriter genre that would come to be known as Americana, these recordings were on a par with Dylan's Basement Tapes or Louis Armstrong's Hot Five and Hot Seven recordings; they were the headwaters of a powerful river of music.

At this point in the saga, Hancock had already released half a dozen or so albums on his own Rainlight label and produced a syndicated live music show from Austin, *Dixie's Bar and Bus Stop*. Gilmore had released his first two albums on the Hightone label. *Rolling Stone* magazine would name him Country Artist of the Year the following year in the wake of his third album, *After Awhile*. And Ely's career was long since well launched. Nineteen ninety would mark his return to the MCA label and see the release of one of his best-selling and best-received albums, *Live at Liberty Lunch*.

All three men, in other words, had momentum in their

own careers to varying degrees. As one critic noted, "They were household names in certain households," a remark reminiscent of Ponty Bone's gentle gibe about "small circles of good taste." The release by Rounder of the Flatlanders tracks, while gratifying, didn't really change anything from their perspective.

But then something happened that did.

* * *

There is no returning, the seasons don't end
They just blow thru the branches and bend with the wind

"South Wind of Summer"
THE FLATLANDERS

It was 1997, maybe early '98, and Joe Ely was in what was probably the last place on earth he wanted to be—the office of a Nashville record executive.

It could have been worse. The executive in question was Tony Brown, who was the head of MCA's country division. Brown wasn't just a suit. The North Carolina native was a musician himself, having toured with no less than Elvis before joining Emmylou Harris's Hot Band.

As a producer and label honcho, Brown had a particular affinity for Texas acts. He had helped propel the careers of Lyle Lovett, Nanci Griffith, Steve Earle, Rodney Crowell, and George Strait to hit albums and new heights. But, like everyone else in the business, he was snakebit when it came to Ely. He just couldn't find the key that would unlock all that potential. It was the same old story.

Brown and Ely were talking about Ely's forthcoming album, *Twistin' in the Wind*. (As it happened, it would be Joe's last recording for the label.)

In the meantime, there was this interesting little tangent...

"Tony comes in with a woman and says, 'This is Kathy Nelson. She'd like you to do a song for Robert Redford's new movie. Interested?'" as Ely recalled it.

Nelson was one of the two music supervisors on Redford's new film, *The Horse Whisperer*, an adaptation of the 1995 Nicholas Evans best-selling novel about a traumatized girl, a truculent horse, a lonely wife, and the cowboy "horse whisperer," an equine healer who redeems them all. It was sensitive as all get-out.

The soundtrack, to be released on MCA, was an Americana hit parade, featuring original tracks from Dwight Yoakam, Lucinda Williams, the Mavericks, Emmylou Harris, Steve Earle, George Strait, Iris DeMent, and more. Ely would be in very good company. He took a copy of the book and went back to Austin.

"I read it and said, yeah, I think I can do something. I started working on it and Tony called me up and says, 'We got a call from Redford's camp. The guy that's working with the music and the album [presumably Nelson's music supervising cohort, John Bissell] knows about your history with the Flatlanders and he has that old album. He says, is there any way you all could get together and do something?' I said, 'I'll ask Butch and Jimmie and see what they think.'"

Twenty-six years gone by, and in the end all it took was a phone call.

"Joe called Butch and me, like, the next day and said, 'Do you guys want to try to do something for the movie?' And we said, 'Sure,'" said Gilmore.

"So we went out to Joe's house and wrote three songs in two days and we loved all of them."

"We were amazed that we actually completed three songs," Hancock said. "We'd never done that before. Jimmie and I had written two or three together, and one of those was over a ten-year period."

"I don't think we had any preconceived notions that we were going to come up with anything," Ely later told *No Depression*. "It was almost like an experiment to see if this works. And we were kind of surprised to see that it actually did."

"Surprise" was an appropriate reaction. Because here's the thing: Despite the decades and the lifelong friendship and the hundreds and hundreds of songs . . . *the Flatlanders had never set out to write together before.*

Even when they had lived together on 14th Street, they'd never sat down and swapped lyrical ideas and put 'em down on paper. "It seemed like every morning someone would wake up and come down to the kitchen table with a new song," said Ely to *Texas Music* magazine. "So we had plenty of new songs to go around. We didn't think we needed to sit down and make up any more together. But in the back of our minds, we always wondered what would happen if we did."

Oh, they'd goofed around together, just long enough to crack each other up (remember "The Longest Song in the World"?), but a sustained, real-life effort at creative collaboration? *Nada*, zip, never.

That first time at Joe's house, they got three keepers: the jaunty, mountain-music-flavored "Down on Filbert's Rise" (the title was a typical Hancockian bit of wordplay), the swinging country-rocker "My Wildest Dreams Grow Wilder Every Day" ("I wake up in the morning, I go to sleep at night / Somewhere in between the two I swear I'll get it right"), and the stately, folk-inflected ballad "The South Wind of Summer."

"My studio became our clubhouse," Ely said. "As soon as we finished a song, we'd put it on tape immediately."

The three recorded "South Wind of Summer" with an eclectic group of Austin musicians that included the invaluable

Lloyd Maines, bluegrass/jazz mandolinist Paul Glasse, the L.A.-meets-Austin rhythm section of drummer Donald Lindley and bassist Glenn Fukunaga, and Chris Gage on piano. Ely produced the session.

Of the three songs, only "South Wind of Summer" wound up on the soundtrack to *The Horse Whisperer*, but it was more than enough to reintroduce the Flatlanders to the world. Fans were astonished and gratified, but no more so than the Flatlanders themselves.

"Probably what made it work was that we'd never done it before," said Hancock. "But we'd been seriously wanting to do it. We'd all been writing songs long enough to trust each other's work and opinions. It's like, check your ego—if you've got any left—at the door, and we'll have a great time."

In May, as the movie was being released, Ely, Hancock, and Gilmore were guests on *Late Night with David Letterman*, performing "South Wind of Summer." That night, after the taping, Gilmore was booked to play a sold-out solo show at the Mercury Lounge. Guess who popped in?

In July 1999, they wound up headlining a show at Central Park's Summerstage series. Hancock opened the show, then joined Gilmore on his set, which preceded Ely's. After Ely's encore, Butch and Jimmie returned to join their compadre for "Dallas, "If You Were a Bluebird," "West Texas Waltz," and Woody Guthrie's "Sowing on the Mountain."

"Nearly four hours after it began," wrote a *No Depression* reviewer, "the concert was over. And as Ely, Gilmore and Hancock left the stage with their arms around each other, it was clear that the oppressive humidity was no match for the strong Texas wind these legendary troubadours brought to New York."

"It was just a big silly loose jam, like any other Flatlanders gig," Hancock told the *Statesman* after the fact. "But it stirred up a bunch of interest. When we got back home we started getting calls from people in other cities wanting us to play their summer festivals, and calls from labels wanting us to make a record."

Robbie Gjersoe, who has played guitar with both the Ely band and the Flatlanders for years, said, "It's like playing with the Beatles. People are in awe wherever they go."

As 2000 dawned, they played four sold-out nights at the Cactus Café in Austin and added a show at Gruene Hall, Texas's oldest dance hall.

Gradually, the one-off gigs began to coalesce into something resembling a tour. But not a "reunion tour."

"It's odd," Gilmore told *Texas Music* magazine, "because from our point of view, we hang out with each other all the time. But for our fans, it's like a real special occasion. But the 'reunion' part of it is somewhat misleading. . . . the band never did break up because we were never together. We were a bunch of friends . . ."

"It's all just sort of falling into place," Hancock told the *Statesman* with his usual irony, "but we hope to do more than just stumble our way through this. Whether we'll live up to or destroy the mystique of the group, who knows? Anytime history gets ruined it's a wonderful thing. But I think we might just be able to create a whole new Flatlanders for the 21st century. Now wouldn't that be weird?"

As for writing together again, after the *Horse Whisperer* sessions . . . Not only yes, but hell yes.

"The main thing that we discovered is that we could do that," said Gilmore. "We worked together real well and loved doing it."

And Ely added, "It's been really fulfilling. It's funny to see all the different trails we've gone out on and then coming back and sitting in a room together and looking at each other and saying, 'Where have we been and what are we gonna talk about?'"

CHAPTER 12

The wind knows how we used to be here now
It circles to remind us all, all about the time we used to spend
If you don't believe in now and then . . . Now it's now again

"Now Again"
THE FLATLANDERS

Alchemy
NOW AGAIN

"It was like, 'Let's do this more often!'" said Joe Ely.

He was talking about writing more songs together. Hancock and Gilmore were all over that idea like ugly on an ape.

As their schedules permitted, over the next year or so, they convened in Ely's studio to hone lyrics and work out harmonies. When the three judged a song a keeper, onto tape it went. The few times in the past that they'd tried to jack around with cowriting, whatever goofy results there were, said Ely, "tended to blow out the window."

There was no advance money on the horizon. Ely paid for the session musicians who worked on the tracks. MCA had been happy to have *The Horse Whisperer* soundtrack, but it wasn't interested in a Flatlanders album (and in fact Ely himself would leave the label not long thereafter).

No record contract, no problem. It gave them elbow room. "We didn't want it to turn into work," said Ely. "It was great that it could be fun without the business getting in the way. There is something unique that only happens when the three of us get together."

Writing together demanded a whole new form of discipline, he said: "We had to resist the urge to write ten-minute songs."

And Butch: "Joe calls it agonizing, but it just seems like we were tuned in to whatever the vibe was, or whatever the song was trying to become. Sometimes we'd have half the song done and realize, oh, no, we've got to throw those lines out. It was totally weird." When the going got tough, he compared the process to "pulling your own teeth."

And Jimmie: "It was a very different kind of writing than we would do as individuals."

The trio and their sidemen laid down fifteen or so tracks, then took them out on the road to see which ones worked in front of an audience and which didn't. They refined harmonies and arrangements on the fly.

"The road really helped us sing together, because we'd do it every night and change the parts," said Ely. "And when we'd come back off the road we'd come in and rerecord the songs again. The road helped the songs come to life.

"We came to realize that each of our voices were so different that when different combinations of them were singing, it made it almost like orchestra instruments. [Performing the songs live] helped us understand who should be singing what parts."

"That was the great experiment of doing a record without a deal," said Gilmore. "And then we went out and toured without any kind of backing or record deal."

"Promoters were baffled," Ely said. "'You don't have a new record?' 'Naw, the last one was thirty years ago.'" Some suggested the new project might ultimately be called *More A Band Than A Legend.*

But at last a little bit of music business juju began rolling the Flatlanders' way.

Just about the time that *The Horse Whisperer* reintroduced the Flatlanders to a new generation, a record label called New West Records opened its doors in Los Angeles and not long thereafter in Austin.

With a carefully curated roster of acclaimed veteran singer/songwriters, young indie upstarts, and alt-country acts, which at times has included Patty Griffin, Steve Earle, Kris Kristofferson, Buddy and Julie Miller, Jim Lauderdale, the Old 97s, John Hiatt, Richard Thompson, the Whigs, and others, the label would seem to be a natural fit for the Flatlanders' idiosyncratic music.

New West thought so, too.

"As the label got more established, there were always rumors that they might get back together and that was incredibly exciting to us because we hoped we could sign them," said Cameron Strang, who was the New West founder and president.

"*The Horse Whisperer* soundtrack fueled the rumors even more. They were doing a performance at, I think, Stubb's, and I came down to Austin. We had the whole Austin office there. We just wanted to do it so badly."

Philosophically, as an executive, he was right in the pocket with the musicians. "The challenge for us with the artists as a label was always, first and foremost, to make the artistic records they wanted to make. The beauty of our company was, and still is, that we're not tied to radio formats. We weren't trying to make records that fit in a certain place."

That was nothing if not the Flatlanders' philosophy.

One thing, said Strang, led to another, "and the guys all agreed New West would be a good home for the band."

So it was that the Flatlanders released *Now Again* on New West in May of 2002, their first new album in three decades.

Did you hear the riddle of a road without a middle,
or an end?

"Yesterday Was Judgment Day"
THE FLATLANDERS

———

"Listen to the time and the timelessness that spans the 30 years between them," wrote Michael Ventura in the *Austin Chronicle* that summer, comparing *Now Again* with the Nashville recordings.

"The younger sound is astonishingly pure and a little distant; the older, gruff and companionable. The younger sound feels effortless; well, nothing people in their fifties do is effortless—the trick is to make the effort spice the music, and the Flatlanders pull that off beautifully. The younger songs are a music of discovery. The older songs are about the price of discovery, and about how discovery isn't enough—you've got to *do* something with what you discover, and that's an entirely different order of difficulty.

"The music of youth is the music of longing. This older (though newer) Flatlanders album is a music of experience. Experience is the one thing in this world you can't fake. Not for long, anyway."

Making the album, Butch told the *Austin American-Statesman*, "was like riding a horse with three saddles."

Ely, having had the most experience in that regard, produced the sessions that yielded the album.

"He really knows the boards and the sound," Gilmore said of Ely, who had also produced his debut album. "He's a phenomenon in that way."

Hancock, of course, couldn't resist his own two cents' worth. "I think the real reason he became producer of the album is because he owned the tape recorder. It's like letting the bass player in the band because he owns the van."

Sometime during the protracted course of the recording, the guys rang up Steve Wesson and Tony Pearson, who had been leading grown-up lives away from music, and told them to grab their musical saw and mandolin and hot-foot it down to Austin to join in the proceedings. The results were gratifying. Having the original five members on the album helped close the circle. Pearson and Wesson would go on to play on all the Flatlanders' subsequent studio recordings.

Twelve of the fourteen songs on the album were credited to "The Flatlanders." The only individual writing credit among the trio belonged to Butch, who brought "Julia" to the table with its basic tracks already recorded.

The scratch studio recordings, Sharon Ely recalled, "turned out to be so good it was almost like the finished product. They didn't have to go back into another studio and record it again. Sometimes when you do that it just wears it out."

The lead-off song on the long-anticipated album by three great songwriters was, perversely, penned by none of them.

"Going Away," with its lyrical components of trains/winds/lost love and its gently swinging front porch groove, sounds like a natural part of the Flatlanders' repertoire. But it was written by Utah Phillips, the political activist and storytelling songwriter who once ran for U.S. Senate on the Peace and Freedom ticket.

"Why not?" said Hancock, invoking the Flatlanders' Prime Directive. "We liked the song." And he added, a little sheepishly, "We don't really know why we do any of those things."

"All of us had been Utah Phillips fans," added Gilmore. "We'd done his songs in the old Flatlanders. So one night we were sitting around, back together again, and trading out songs. I threw that one out, and Butch and Joe had never heard me do it before. And after that, Joe would say, 'Let's work on "Going Away" again.'"

Rolling Stone, in its review in the June 20 issue, cited the band's "more a legend status," but added, "they have a hell of a good time tearing it down.

"The ghosts of their hauntingly beautiful 1972 debut remain . . . but the emphasis this time is all about fun. Hancock and Gilmore hog all the best songs—Hancock's 'Julia' is the real standout—but Ely's production packs all the punch of his live shows. . . . as a devil-may-care hoot, it's one for the ages."

A hoot, sure—you don't have to listen further than the Waylonesque "I Thought the Wreck Was Over" or the hilarious non sequitur of "Pay the Alligator" to get that takeaway—but there was more at work than that.

There are the melodies for one thing; there is time and light and space between the notes, from the lacy guitar-and-mandolin interplay of "Now Is Now Again" to the rubbery walking bass and honky-tonk guitar of "My Wildest Dreams Grow Wilder Every Day" to the tribal chants of the eerie "Down in the Light of the Melon Moon" and the bluegrass breakdown at the conclusion of the rerecorded "The South Wind of Summer" that closes out the album at a canter.

"Rhythm is power," acknowledged Ely to the *Statesman*. "It's a brute force. But there's something in melody that really is magic. I think the wind had a lot to do with forming the melodies out there—because the best melodies are a little windy, you know? They don't stay still."

And there were those lyrics, each of them a three-corner bank shot between restless imaginations.

"Standin' in the station, I got no destination / I'm wavin' my heart goodbye," Jimmie sings, plaintively, against a bouncy, rockabilly-flavored track. "Standin' in the rain, wonderin' if the train / Will stop before the tears will dry."

(Ely must have been tickled by that. "There's nothing more touching, I think, than a really fast, happy melody with real sad lyrics in it," he noted.)

Hancock's love of sardonic, Dylanesque wordplay and alliteration would seem to be the key to "You Make It Look Easy": "Shattered and scattered to the four wild winds / My angels and my devils and a few of my friends / You got 'em all dancin' on the head of a pin / You make it look easy."

But not so fast. "People are always saying, 'I can tell what lines you or Jimmie or Joe wrote,'" Hancock said. "And we might remember a few of those ourselves. But a lot of them took a long, strenuous road to get one line perfected.

"It was like, the funny combination of the three of us—sometimes it would be the two of us working a little harder, and the other one would come in and double-check us and take it to another level.

"When it's one person writing a song, there are still several people inside your head arguing. Joe figured out that there wasn't just three of us writing, there were about nine of us writing."

Or, as he is fond of saying, *The things we go through to go through the things we go through* . . .

> Put me on the hot seat, put me on the spot
> Tell me I'm in trouble or tell me I'm not
> It feels so good it might be right where I belong

"Right Where I Belong"
THE FLATLANDERS

———

The reaction to the reappearance of the Flatlanders would have, as Dan Jenkins once wrote, gratified an Egyptian mummy.

The album went to the Top 20 of the *Billboard* Country Chart, and stayed on the chart for twenty-two weeks. Letterman had them back on, this time with Tom Cruise. They taped an episode of the iconic music series *Austin City Limits*. The Americana bible *No Depression* put them on the cover of the magazine. Hell, even the *Wall Street Journal* liked the album.

But perhaps the most improbable cheerleader for the group was that professional curmudgeon, radio host Don Imus.

According to the Music Industry News Network website, "Since the band's first appearance on his show [*Imus in the Morning*] June 19, Don Imus has totally embraced the band's music, telling his audience continuously how much he liked the album and even going on Larry King's CNN talk show to shout its praises." Imus went on to offer ten thousand dollars to the chosen charity of the first major radio station to land *Now Again* in the Top 10.

"Imus played a huge role in that first Flatlanders album," said Cameron Strang. "He played that record all the time. He was just a massive supporter."

(After one Flatlanders appearance on his show, Imus turned to his engineer off mike and said, "I love Jimmie Dale Gilmore! I may be thirty years too late, but Jesus Christ that's great shit.")

Hancock, Gilmore, and Ely repaid the shout-out by taking time out from the southwestern leg of their tour to visit and play for the children at the Imus Ranch northeast of Santa Fe. The operation, a four-thousand-acre working cattle ranch designed to give young cancer patients and siblings of SIDs victims a taste of the cowboy West and instill self-sufficiency, is only one of Imus's and his wife Deidre's charitable endeavors, although arguably it's the one closest to his heart.

Maybe Imus, the old crank, was dialed in to the sheer amount of fun that Jimmie, Joe, and Butch had in making the album. *No Depression* wrote, "The trio exudes a spirit of camaraderie that suggests that no one could have as much fun listening to the music as these guys had recording it."

"Pay the Alligator" is a case in point, perhaps the goofiest lyric any of the three has ever put his name to. Riffing on an offhand comment by Gilmore in the studio about a malfunctioning bathroom radiator, the three came up with a *Looney Tunes*–style cautionary tale fueled by a contagious Chet Atkins/Chuck Berry guitar lick.

"It sounds like something you'd hear your grandfather say," Ely told *No Depression*. "If you don't watch out, you're gonna have to pay the alligator."

Set that lark against the magisterial, magical-realist midnight landscape of the haunting "Down in the Light of the Melon Moon," measure all the musical moods and textures in between, and one gets a true sense of the vision, nerve, and scope of *Now Again*.

CHAPTER 13

This is a Joe Ely song that Butch Hancock wrote,
and I'm gonna sing it!

JIMMIE DALE GILMORE
onstage

Cruising Speed
WHEELS OF FORTUNE AND LIVE '72

To hear Joe Ely tell it, the Flatlanders were shit-hot, coming off extended national tours to promote *Now Again*.

"We were on a roll," he said. "The band had gotten really good. We got back from a tour and I said, 'Let's just go into the studio right now and just record songs. Let's just keep working.' So we recorded for about two weeks, right off the road."

Those sessions, over twenty songs in all, eventually yielded 2004's *Wheels of Fortune*, the second album from the Flatlanders' modern incarnation. (Reminded that F. Scott Fitzgerald famously said that there are no second acts in American lives, Jimmie Dale Gilmore cracked up laughing: "Except we never really had a first act!")

The guys in the touring band (Robbie Gjersoe, guitar; Joel Guzman, accordion; Gary Herman, bass; and Chris Searles, drums) concurred. Tony Pearson and Steve Wesson were brought back on board. Jazz/rock guitarist Mitch Watkins (who'd originally recorded with Ely during the *Hi-Res* days) was recruited, and Lloyd Maines, as much a Flatlander as anyone, added pedal steel and Dobro.

Wheels of Fortune differed from its predecessor in significant ways. Individual songwriters were credited this time around. The tracks were hotter, more rocking than almost anything on *Now Again*. And, most significantly, instead of filling the album with all-new material, Gilmore, Hancock, and Ely dipped into their respective back catalogs. Some of the tunes dated back to the dawn of their respective careers.

Part of the rationale for that decision was to air out songs they had written but never recorded, or that were underexposed. Additionally, each of the three wanted to try out songs by the others.

"I said, 'I gotta go back and relearn some of these songs!'" exclaimed Hancock, perhaps speaking of "Eggs of Your Chickens," "Wheels of Fortune," "Wishin' for You," and "Once Followed by the Wind," several of which dated back to the late seventies.

"Indian Cowboy" was a tragic circus story song dating from Ely's Ringling Bros. days that he had pretty much forgotten about until he heard it recorded by Townes Van Zandt and Guy Clark. He also had three more unrecorded ones, "Back to My Old Molehill," the cartoonish "I'm Gonna Strangle You Shorty," and "Neon of Nashville."

Jimmie reprised his mournful "Deep Eddy Blues" and the transcendent "See the Way" from his 1989 solo album. The stark heads-up of "You've Got to Go to Sleep Alone" ("Even if you're lying with somebody you really love / Still you've got to go to sleep alone") and the ominous blues-rocker, "Midnight Train"—think Elmore James meets Robert Johnson at the crossroads—both dated from his 1991 *After Awhile* album.

"Whistle Blues" was another arrow from the quiver of their

old Lubbock amigo Al Strehli, done up here as an Elvis/Doc Pomus–style rocker.

"See the Way," a rare cowrite between Butch and Jimmie, may be the album's highlight.

It's as pure a distillation of the guys' guiding tenets from Eastern philosophy as they have ever penned, namely, that you can only achieve completion and fulfillment by letting everything go:

> *You're gonna be sad till you stop hurtin'*
> *For the sake of findin' peace of mind*
> *Rise up from there, throw back the curtain*
> *That covers your heart and makes you blind*
> *See the way true love has left you*
> *For a lie that you must feed*
> *See the way true love has left you*
> *For what you want but just don't need*

It's a lament but also a promise. A way forward couched in a weary dance hall shuffle. Imagine the Bhagavad Gita boiled down by Hank Williams and playing at D-16 on the jukebox at the He's Not Here Lounge in Wichita Falls and you get the picture.

"When I was much younger, I had a really dark spot about my music," said Gilmore to a *Statesman* reporter. "I worried that I might not be able to make a living in music, even though it was the only thing I cared about. And this old friend of mine said, 'Imagine the meanest old drunken cowboy you could ever meet, anywhere, in a bar. You know what? There's a song, somewhere, that brings tears to his eyes.'" "See the Way" might just be that song.

The raid-the-pantry approach of *Wheels of Fortune* had both its fans and its detractors out in the wider world.

The reviewer for the website AllMusic.com said, "There isn't anything outwardly wrong with *Wheels of Fortune*, which boasts solid craftsmanship from front to back, but while *Now Again* sounded like a spirited collaboration between three unique but complementary talents, this album feels more like the work of three talented friends sharing some studio time— the results are pleasing, but they fall noticeably short of what these guys are capable of."

John Morthland, on the other hand, writing for *No Depression*, said, "I eventually found [*Now Again*] lacked sufficient staying power. The same won't happen with *Wheels of Fortune*. These songs have depth and breadth. . . . I can't help but think that's because they didn't triple co-write, as they did the last time, and so none of the tunes are softened by the too-many-cooks syndrome. . . . Some of the best performances come on songs written by someone other than the lead singer."

You pays your money, in other words, and you takes your choice.

Peter Jesperson, New West's Vice-President of Production and Catalog, said *Wheels of Fortune* is his personal favorite of the Flatlanders' three contemporary studio albums.

"It's just the one that moves me most," he said. "When they began laying the groundwork for the album, they went back to what they did best, simply singing each other's songs with great enthusiasm: Joe singing Jimmie's 'Midnight Train,' Butch singing Jimmie's 'Deep Eddy Blues,' Jimmie singing Joe's 'Back to My Old Molehill,' and so on."

There are a lot of moods to choose from on *Wheels of Fortune*, from the cinematic pathos that is "Indian Cowboy" to the loping Buddy Holly/Bobby Fuller West Texas–style romp of "Back to My Old Molehill," which features one of Gilmore's best everything-happens-to-me mock laments: "We were flyin' too high for each other / Too high for our own good will / I wish you would take me off of this mountain / Back to my old molehill."

Then there's Hancock's folk-flavored, buy-one-metaphor-get-five-free "Eggs of Your Chickens," which riffs on love, war, karma, wind, mountains, roads, and, yep, chickens. He's more serious, but no less allusive, on the title song: "The fires of love I've lit have turned to ashes / And now they're only smolderin' at my feet." Gilmore's lead vocal on the track is a thing of carefully crafted beauty.

Ely's "Neon of Nashville" is something like a Truman Capote short story boiled down to five minutes; the rise and fall of a mythical beauty who might almost have been a product of collective yearning. Maines's steel, reined in with a firm hand, adds a sadly sweet instrumental counterpoint.

Though they did not collaborate on songwriting this time around, give-and-take was still the order of the day.

"Everybody brings a little different story to the table," said Hancock. "A little different musical sense, a little more daring here, a little less daring there. It's a sculpture. Or you hope it's not a horse that turns into a camel."

The One Knite Dive and Tavern, as it was formally known, was a dark, dank, wonderfully forbidden place. Patrons entered by walking through the frame of an upright coffin. The cluttered *objets de junque* hanging from the ceiling— old kitchen sinks, bicycle tires, mangled appliances—sent up warning flags that this was not a joint for the meek or the faint of heart.

From *Stevie Ray Vaughan: Caught in the Crossfire*, by JOE NICK PATOSKI and BILL CRAWFORD

Wheels of Fortune was not the only Flatlanders album to be released in 2004. By happy circumstance, through a circuitous route, a vintage tape of the group in performance in Austin was released by New West the same year. *Live at the One Knite/ June 8th 1972* (aka *Live '72*) is more akin to a field recording than a proper live album, but it is a snapshot of the original group in the wake of its Nashville pilgrimage that is as valuable for its archival qualities as its musical appeal.

At first blush, the One Knite was the last place you'd expect to find a genteel acoustic ensemble like the Flatlanders. The place wore its dive bar status proudly on its sleeve.

Its locale, which today is sprouting condos, trendy clubs, and craft cocktail bars, was at the time host to an ice factory, an array of junk stores, a Mexican food café or two, and other marginal enterprises. Hookers, drunks, and junkies prowled the side streets and alleys and the Waller Creek bottomlands around the club's downtown Red River Street location. All this right around the corner from the Austin police station.

Inside the funky antique limestone building, electric blues roared from the stage, turning the packed, sweaty crowd into one, hot churning pudding of humanity.

Storm, featuring a hot-shit guitarist named Jimmie Vaughan, ruled the roost on Blue Mondays. Jimmie was in the vanguard of a bevy of young, white Dallas blues musicians who came south to mix it up with the native bluesmen from Austin's East Side. Jimmie's little brother Stevie was making a mark every Tuesday with the Nightcrawlers, and Angela Strehli, whose "The Heart You Left Behind" was covered by the Flatlanders, rocked the house on Wednesday nights with her integrated R&B band, Southern Feelings.

The migration included other Dallasites who would become fixtures in the Texas blues scene, including Paul Ray (with his great band, the Cobras), Denny Freeman (who would go on to play with Bob Dylan), and the late, great drummer/songwriter/vocalist Doyle Bramhall.

The sharp-dressed R&B cats were in distinct contrast to the cowboy-hatted hippie country-rockers who were becoming the public face of Austin music. "We didn't give a shit about any of that," said Jimmie Vaughan. "We just wanted to play blues and listen to our Lazy Lester records."

But before the blues hounds took over the scene, the One Knite had hosted quieter acts like the white country blues guitarist Bill Neely, country singer Cody Hubach, and Kenneth Threadgill, who could yodel like Jimmie Rodgers. "Joey" Ely, Jimmie, and John X. Reed (Lubbock ex-pats all) also made the cut.

Everyone, solo acts and bands alike, played for no cover, pass the hat.

One Knite co-owner Gary Oliver took over the place in 1970 with two partners, Roger "One Knite" Collins and Roddy Howard.

"It was actually owned by some law students and business students who bought it in the late sixties, basically so they could drink there," recalled Collins.

Oliver booked the acts for five years, and he also got into the habit of recording many of the bands that graced the hot, crowded, tiny stage.

"I recorded by hauling in my old reel-to-reel and hanging mikes from the ceiling joists in between all the junk," he said. "The big challenge, apart from wild swings in band volume, was protecting the tape deck from stumbling drunks and tipping pitchers."

That was the backdrop of the Flatlanders' summer 1972 performance at the venue. Tony Pearson recalled its being an on-the-spot pickup gig ("There was no band there, but there was a stand-up bass onstage. Everybody had their guitars, so we said, 'We'll play!'"). He also recalled Butch ducking out for some reason early in the show, and indeed there are no lead Hancock vocals on the resulting album.

The set list, typical for its time, is a fascinating glimpse into the Flatlanders' eclectic influences: a couple of Townes songs ("Tecumseh Valley" and "Waitin' Around to Die"); some folk/blues standards ("San Francisco Bay Blues," "Hesitation Blues"); a back porch take on Blind Lemon Jefferson's salacious "Long Snake Moan"; some Hank ("Honky-Tonk Blues," "Settin' the Woods on Fire") and Dylan ("Walkin' down the Line"); their fave Cajun cover, "Jole Blon"; and, just to mess with people's heads, a slow, stately take on Sam Cooke's "Bring It on Home to Me."

Only a couple of songs by Butch ("You've Never Seen Me Cry" and "Stars in My Life") and by Al Strehli ("So I'll Run" and "I Know You") reflected the Flatlanders' original repertoire. It was clearly a cover-heavy set catering to the fifteen or twenty beer-drinking yahoos in attendance. You can hear every single one of them yammering throughout. Quiet, worshipful contemplation was not the habitual demeanor of One Knite audiences.

In 2003, a local record producer named Jim Yanaway acquired the tapes from Oliver and got them to the guys, according to Butch's recollection, and thence to New West.

It was a loosey-goosey project all the way around, but there was a certain honesty that permeated the recording and the performance. "I always liked this [recording], even though it is so ragged," said Gilmore. "In a certain way, it's truer to the way we really were than the studio recordings."

Ely liked the fact that the album saw the light of day simply because he thought these were the only "real" Flatlanders recording outstanding. "We thought that was the only thing that existed beside the Nashville tape," he explained.

"It wasn't a good-sounding tape—you could hear the audience as much as the band—but we thought it was the only thing that existed from that era."

"What the Flatlanders are at this point," said a review in *No Depression*, "is loose. . . . But the intensity and the knowing playfulness that these gents bring to blues not touched by the folkies shows just how they were something else again.

"The Flatlanders in 1972, finally, sound pretty much like you might expect—a little loopy, offering sweet, smart fun. This disc is more a treat than a revelation, and there's nothing wrong with that."

Once the Odessa Tapes were released in 2012, the band and their fans had a much better representation of a classic Flatlanders performance, thus eclipsing this set. Still, the One Knite tapes are a ragged-but-right souvenir of a hot, sweaty night in Austin with the five Flatlanders playing for the sheer fun of it.

CHAPTER 14

For everything this world is worth
We're all just migrants on this Earth
Returning to the dust from where we came.

"Homeland Refugee"
FLATLANDERS

Dust to Dust

HILLS AND VALLEYS

"When I listen to this music it's like looking into an old ranch-er's eyes. You can look into that rancher's face and see those lines, and know that he's been around the block. What these three guys have done on this record is taken everything they've lived, everything they've learned, and written it down."

Thus did Lloyd Maines describe to the *Statesman* 2009's *Hills and Valleys*, the third of the Flatlanders' studio albums for New West.

Maines was anything but a disinterested observer in this case. For the first time on a modern Flatlanders project, Joe Ely surrendered the producer's chair. The natural candidate to sit behind the board was, all agreed, their old friend and band-mate from Lubbock.

Leaving aside his considerable instrumental prowess on pedal steel and an array of other instruments, Maines brought unimpeachable producer's chops to the table. He won a

Grammy in 2003 for his production of the Dixie Chicks' multi-platinum album *Home*.

Beginning with his production work on Terry Allen's 1976 debut *Juarez* and Allen's groundbreaking follow-up *Lubbock (on everything)*, Lloyd secured a production credit on a virtual Murderer's Row of Texas musicians: Jerry Jeff Walker, Robert Earl Keen, Pat Green, Ray Wylie Hubbard, Two Tons of Steel, the Maines Brothers Band, Bruce and Charlie Robison, and Terri Hendrix, with whom he has also recorded and toured for over fifteen years. And he had produced solo projects by Jimmie and Butch, in addition to his tenure as a pivotal member of several iterations of the Joe Ely Band.

Sometimes it seems like every kid in Texas with a guitar and a demo tape in hand is looking for Maines to turn the knobs on his or her future masterpiece.

Self-taught in the studio, Maines nonetheless has evolved an elastic technique that suits itself to the client of the moment.

"I'm pretty much a real hands-on guy," he told *Performing Songwriter* magazine. "If I'm producing an already existing band, I'll sit back and let it take its course, and if I feel that it might have been better if it had made a different turn, I'll definitely speak up and present my case. I'll try to take whatever route they're going and optimize it, to make it as good as it can be. If an artist has a real definite idea about what they want their song to be, I don't really give much resistance, I just try to vibe in and try to optimize their ideas. But I always have pretty good luck with that."

His history with the Flatlanders and his simpatico production style made him the natural go-to guy when Ely tired of the producer's role.

As producer on the previous albums, "Joe spent five times as much time as any of the rest of us," said Gilmore. "He's a workaholic anyway, but still . . . I think it just got suggested one day that Lloyd do it."

"Joe might have wanted to concentrate more on the music and not try to organize the whole picture," suggested Hancock. "And Lloyd was someone we could trust completely. He's right in the center of all our music."

Ely didn't put up a fight. "It kind of freed me up to not have to take care of the details," he said. "We recorded everything in my studio before Lloyd came in. Then I gave him those tracks to show how the songs should go, and he put his magic on it—dusted stuff off and cut things up."

"Joe called me and said, 'We feel like we've got some really good songs together, but sometimes I get too close to it and can't stay objective, and we all trust you,'" Maines said.

As the *Statesman* story recounted, Maines suggested changes to the keys of several finished songs to open them up for richer harmonies. He also moved the acoustic instruments to the forefront in place of the electric guitars that prowled *Wheels of Fortune*.

Lloyd also moved the band out of the "clubhouse" of Ely's home studio and into an isolated top-shelf studio called The Zone, outside of Austin in Dripping Springs.

"When you're dealing with three personalities like that, you just try to capture what they're doing. We never talked about a new direction; we just let the songs dictate."

The songs, in turn, were inspired in part by what was happening out in what some folks laughingly call the real world.

To put it mildly, everything was going to hell in a handbasket.

In the four or so years since *Wheels of Fortune* was released, Hurricane Katrina drowned New Orleans, the wars in Iraq and Afghanistan raged unabated, the global economy went over a cliff and the stock market melted down, a Pacific tsunami killed a quarter of a million people, wildfires ravaged California, and the American Dream seemed to recede permanently out of reach for millions.

Depending on where you stood on the political spectrum,

the election of Barack Obama in 2008 was either the one bright spot in the litany of doom, or one more catastrophe to add to the list.

The Flatlanders had never flaunted their politics in song, which is one reason their music remains timeless. The one song that speaks most specifically to a cultural era, "Bhagavad Decreed" (which they did not write), sounds painfully dated to these ears.

But some things hit too close to home.

"The first official night we were working together [on songs for the new album], Katrina happened," recalled Gilmore. "When the economic crash happened, we were in the studio."

Living in Terlingua, a stone's throw from Mexico, Hancock and his wife Adrienne watched in dismay as angry Anglo nativists demonized illegal immigrants and a clamor arose for a border fence across La Frontera (a ludicrous notion in that particular stretch of Texas).

So when they sat down together they found some newsworthy—and deeply affecting—subject matter that lent itself to their efforts.

"'After the Storm' was about Katrina," said Gilmore. The images of devastation and displacement in the song are still raw and bleeding years later.

"Borderless Love" used the real-life border fence to advocate against fear, the ultimate cage: "A wall is a mirror that can only reveal / One side of a story that passes for real / But break it all down, it all becomes clear / It's the fearless who love and the loveless who fear."

In that context, the band's cover of Woody Guthrie's "Sowing on the Mountain," with its biblical imagery of judgment, fit right in. Guthrie was a natural-born Flatlander anyway.

He would certainly approve of what many listeners believe to be the album's centerpiece—the set-opening "Homeland Refugee."

The lyrics, set against a luminous folk-flavored melody redolent with mandolin and Tex-Mex accordion, turn Woody's Depression-era Okies bound for California's promised land on their heads. In the song, heartbreakingly, the grandchildren of those migrants have gone bust themselves in the modern Great Recession, and there's nothing left to do but limp back to the barren landscapes their forefathers fled:

> *I lost my home when the deal went bust*
> *To the so-called security and trust*
> *I planned my life the way they said I should*
> *. . . Now I'm leaving California for the Dust Bowl*
> *They took it all, there's nowhere else to go*
> *The pastures of plenty are burning by the sea*
> *And I'm just a homeland refugee*

"Homeland Refugee"
THE FLATLANDERS

———

"It's not a song of uplift," said the late music journalist Chet Flippo, "but of a will to survive."

For this album, the Flatlanders returned to the collaboration model that served them well on *Now Again*.

But having done so once previously didn't automatically make the process easier this time around.

"It's not easy writing together," said Ely to the *Statesman*. "And sometimes it's not even fun. Sometimes, it was hair-pulling hard. One day we sat together for six hours without saying a word. And at the end of it we said, 'I guess we're snakebit. Let's get out of here.'"

"I still disagree with anybody that says they know how to write their songs," said Hancock, desperate to avoid overthinking it. "I believe there's a mystery beyond any comprehension. People may have specific techniques, formulas, whatever, but they still don't know *how* it happens.

"All of us, having heard hundreds of thousands of songs, we have a good idea of how a song works: there's a beginning, an end, and weird stuff happens in the middle. I mean, that's basically it."

Cole Porter could not have said it better.

But, he added, "Songwriting is fascinating to me because it's a great example of what life is like. From one moment to the next, you don't know where your consciousness is going to be. Songs are just a reflection of the mind. The whole point of art, the whole point of life, is that anything is possible."

The trio wrote eight of the thirteen songs on the album (besides the Woody Guthrie track, the only cover is the rocking, reeling "The Way We Are," by Gilmore's son, Colin). Ely penned "Love's Own Chains." "Thank God for the Road," by Butch, is a distillation of Hancock's lifelong the-journey-is-the-destination perspective ("It's an arrow and it's a snake / It's asleep and it's awake / And it stretches from the cradle to the grave").

"When we're writing together," said Gilmore, "it's just like it's always been. We bring different things to it and affect each other in surprising ways."

"Joe describes it as, we all go off traveling in different directions and come back in and it's like unloading the backpack," Hancock said. "'Look what I felt or saw or thought!'"

"It's like pulling teeth sometimes for days on end, but the collaboration between us is interesting and fun," said Gilmore. "The things that pop up as we're messing with a song can be something so hilarious or so beautiful. But lot of it is, we need to finish this verse. And we all need to come up with something that we all will settle on. It's work. But it's fun work."

Fun indeed. Consider this exchange (from a 2009 *Statesman* article) on the creation of the mind-bending, tongue-tangling love song "No Way I'll Never Need You":

Jimmie: I had the feeling, when we started, that this is a good idea, but I don't think we could make anything of it. (Laughter)

Joe: Sometimes we'd write no more than two lines to that song the whole day. I remember walking out of the studio feeling like I was tied up in knots. (More laughter)

Butch: The first day or two I was thinking, "How am I going to tell Joe this is a bad idea?" (Hearty laughter)

Jimmie: I don't remember exactly what got said or done, but something happened. And all of a sudden I said to myself, "This is going to be a great song."

Talk of settling the inevitable (at least to an outsider) disagreements over a lyric or an arrangement also sets the three to chuckling. To paraphrase the action movie trope, head-butting is not an option. As they told me in separate interviews:

Jimmie: It's almost like we're telepathic or something. We can just kind of tell when something's not working.

Butch: Usually any decision is always made with the realization that it can easily be overridden two minutes later. It's tentative till it's done and we all feel good about it.

Joe: When the three of us get together it's pretty evident what's going to work and what's not. (Sharon Ely laughed at this gem of understatement.) Because we know each other, and when things don't work we know it immediately. Sometimes it's like two words in one line that don't work and it takes six months to find the right two words.

Sooner or later it's now or never

"Just About Time"
FLATLANDERS

———

There is as much metaphysics as topical here-and-now in the tracks of *Hills and Valleys*, perhaps more.

"Free the Wind," for instance, encapsulates an ethos that is as much a piece of the West Texas Jesus the Flatlanders grew up with as their own evolving Buddhist spirituality: "From wanting happiness for others / Comes all the joy the world contains / From wanting pleasure for yourself / Comes only sorrow, only pain."

The honky-tonking "Just About Time," complete with Steve Wesson's saw-warbling counterpoint to the vocals and a Jerry Lee–style piano by Bukka Allen (Terry's son), manages the neat trick of turning the whole cosmos on its ear: "Some are denying it's just about time / Some don't believe in space / If you try to undo what's done been did / You'll mistake the static for the thrill of the chase." Take that, Stephen Hawking.

Journalist Brad Buchholz, who has written a great deal of graceful prose about the Flatlanders over the years, said of *Hills and Valleys*: "At its core, the album . . . considers humanity and humility, our preposterous smallness in a vast world, the idea of interconnection, the possibility of love, the breath of creation, the spiritual power of the journey. Impermanence. It's a word that's never uttered on *Hills and Valleys*. Yet it's the breeze that ripples over every song."

The tracks, said *Esquire* magazine, musically blend "Texas swing [and] Appalachian bluegrass and [filter them] through a layer of *norteño*, the jubilant dance-hall music of the Tex-Mex borderlands."

No Depression called the record a "song cycle of broken dreams, heartsick vagabonds and populist resilience—songs that are steeped in the spirit of Woody Guthrie yet are as timely as tomorrow's foreclosure. . . . 'Free the Wind' and Ely's closing 'There's Never Been' are more like secular hymns, with the spiritual delicacy of haikus. . . . This release finally convinces that the whole is more than the sum of its considerable parts."

The Flatlanders will never be confused with CNN or Fox News. But Ely defended the infusion of headline events into the band's music.

"Our songs were [habitually] more romantic—the sun, wind, and moon—and more spiritual with songs like 'Stars in My Life,'" he said. "And kind of funny in a cosmically twisted kind of way.

"But it seems like when we started *Hills and Valleys*, the stock market fell, we watched New Orleans, one of our favorite cities, drown and so many things, the elections and the wars. . . . It's a topical period of time, I think.

"And because we were sitting down and writing at the time, everything seemed to rub off on us. But I don't see it as topical; it's more the story of where we are."

CHAPTER 15

*It's just like these three guys to record what is, to my ears,
their greatest album, and then forget it ever existed.*

MICHAEL VENTURA,
in the liner notes to *The Odessa Tapes*

Closing the Circle

THE ODESSA TAPES

It was 2002 and Sylvester Rice was not in a good place.

The Flatlanders fan who had helped pave their way to Nashville and played bass on those Music City sessions was mortally ill with lung cancer. He needed money, perhaps to pay for medical expenses. And he thought he knew of some collateral, some dusty boxes of recording tape that had been sitting on the top shelf of his bedroom closet for decades.

Long removed from the music scene, he nevertheless still had a few connections. He picked up the phone and rang up an old buddy from the Caldwell Studio days.

"He called me and said, 'I've been keeping these masters for all these years, but I don't know if they'll play,'" said Lloyd Maines. "He couldn't even remember for sure if they'd been recorded in Odessa or Big Spring."

Rice asked Maines if he could at least send the tapes down to Lloyd in Austin so Maines could see if there was anything there. Maines was not optimistic; polyester recording tape tends to deteriorate over time. To restore it, you have to basically bake it in a convection oven to get the moisture out, and the results can be uncertain. But he said, sure, send 'em on.

When Maines got the tapes, he saw written on the box "three track recordings," which was archaic technology by that time. What the hell. He took them to his home base, Cedar Creek Studios, and threaded a reel onto a half-inch two-track machine. He'd at least be able to hear all three tracks, albeit somewhat out of proportion.

"It was the kind of tape that was not polyester, but more like acetate, so it wasn't ruined," Maines said. "And it played like a champ! It sounded *amazing*. The clarity of Jimmie's voice, the overall thing, I could tell it was really good."

Maines made a safety CD copy of the tapes—he wasn't certain the antiques would play more than once—and called Rice back in Lubbock.

"I told him they sounded great and what did he want to do? He said, 'I have no idea.'

"He said, 'I paid for the [Odessa] session and never got paid back, because when Shelby Singleton got involved, I got edged out of any kind of money deal.'"

Rice said he'd like for the Flatlanders to have the tapes back, but he'd like some reimbursement.

"I called Joe and said, 'You've got to hear these tapes. You're not gonna believe how good this thing sounds.' He barely remembered doing it."

"I told Lloyd, 'I remember those tapes and they weren't very good,'" Ely said. "And he said, 'No, they sound really, really good.' So I got with Lloyd and listened to them, and I agreed. That's when I told Butch and Jimmie. Sylvester was not in good health, so we bought the tapes from him so he could pay his medical bills."

"They ponied up," Maines said. Although he doesn't recall the exact amount the guys paid, he described it as quite a bit. "It was a nice gesture on their part."

Lloyd was the bagman.

"I took those masters and Jimmie brought me a cashier's check made out to Syl. I met him like a big covert deal at a Barnes & Noble, handed him a paper sack with the tapes, and he gave me the check."

Ely searched high and low before finding a functioning three-track tape machine at the Capitol Records studios in Los Angeles, where he was able to transfer the masters to a modern format. The Capitol engineer asked him where he'd found the tapes, and Ely replied, oh, they've been on a closet shelf in Lubbock, Texas, for thirty years. The engineer just laughed. "We spend millions a year to keep our tapes in vaults, and these look in perfect shape," he said.

The purity of the music astonished the three musicians. It was an instant time machine.

"The Odessa Tapes came out of nowhere," Ely said. "It was a big surprise. We thought those tapes were long gone. But we were extremely pleased to find them, because it really captured that 14th Street sitting-around-the-table feel. It's a great slice of that era and it's really precious. I cherish that tape, because it's exactly what we sounded like in 1972."

"The first time I heard it, I was amazed," said Gilmore. "I was expecting crackles and hisses, like an old 78. But the aural quality and the performances amaze me. It just sounded like us. You hear the flaws in it—the bass goes wacky and stuff, but never in a way that ruins it. I was listening to the tapes out at Joe's house and [songwriter] Kimmie Rhodes was there, too. She leaned over to me and said, 'You don't sound any different!'"

Gilmore wondered aloud about the Flatlanders' funny back-assward karma, the kind of career trajectory that caused the *New York Times* to call them "a supergroup in reverse."

"The Flatlanders always had things that went wrong in certain respects," he said. "But then things would go right for us in odd ways. Like finding this tape."

For Hancock, the songs took him back to his tractor-driving days, when he first started writing songs and they seemed to jump out of his guitar one after the other. "Shadow of the Moon," he recalled, was born in May of 1971, and "One Road More" was from December. During the summer, between those two benchmarks, he first performed his masterpiece, "If You Were a Bluebird," on the roof of the 14th Street house.

"We didn't get into the music for the business," he told *Nashville Scene*. "We got into it for the music and the sheer wonder of it all."

"We were ecstatic when we realized what these were and what we had," said New West's Peter Jesperson. "That Nashville record was a big deal, but it's more forced, not as natural as the Odessa Tapes. I thought every one of the songs that were done later in Nashville was done better on the Odessa recordings. It was a Holy Grail kind of thing."

Tony Pearson, who played mandolin on both the Odessa and Nashville recordings, echoed Jesperson's assessment of the two sessions.

"To me, the original Odessa one is the real Flatlanders," he said. "That's what we sounded like. The innocence and the simplicity that is so important in that first recording is missing [in later Flatlanders records]. Naïveté, at least to me, is an essential component of all that was Flatlanders. That lasted a short time and then it was gone.

"Jimmie, Joe, and Butch have gone on to create so much more as individuals. They put words and music together as only they can. Maybe the Flatlanders ended in Odessa. But it really doesn't much matter, as long as those guys keep making music."

They have not lost their freshness or their ability to surprise, perhaps because they have not lost their capacity to
be surprised.

MICHAEL VENTURA,
in the liner notes to *The Odessa Tapes*

The Odessa Tapes was released on August 28, 2012, to great acclaim by fans and critics alike.

The package itself was gorgeous: a black trifold design made
up to resemble an old photo album with a Polaroid-style photo
of a lonely windmill regarding the sweeping plains as cumulus
clouds drift serenely overhead.

Photos abound inside, too, most of them candid and previously unseen. One stands out—Ely in a gimme cap, playing
guitar and grinning on the back porch of some farmhouse. It's
a party, clearly, with some folks opening cold beers and others
dancing (there's a pretty girl in cutoffs, her back to the camera,
who might be Sharon Ely). Kids are hanging on the edge of
the makeshift stage, and everyone is clearly having a hell of a
good time . . . making their own fun under the West Texas sky.
Nothin' else to do.

A perceptive, moving essay by Michael Ventura serves
as liner notes. Who better? He's known these guys for four
decades.

An accompanying DVD featuring an interview with the
band rounded out the package.

The music inside was a revelation; warm, intimate, assured,
balanced (Steve Wesson's saw, which had been rudely shoved
to the front in the Nashville mix, was properly relegated to
background texture and an occasional solo here). The guitars, mandolin, and Dobro ripple like artesian springwater.
The harmonies are more in evidence, the give-and-take more
pronounced.

"These old-but-new recordings reveal the Flatlanders as that missing link on the road from Hank Williams to Wilco," said NPR radio host David Brown, who produced a one-hour special on the making of the album. "This is the definitive beginning of a legacy."

The *Nashville Scene* asked, "Is it possible to be a supergroup in retrospect?"

American Songwriter gave the album four out of five stars and said, "The songs sound startlingly fresh and new. In fact, the sound, singing, and arrangements are livelier, more direct and more passionate than the Nashville versions of the same songs. . . . Gilmore's lead singing seems more forcefully upfront and confident, yet still is full of the sweet, lonesome gentleness that is his trademark."

In a concert review, the *Chicago Tribune* noted "the casual chemistry between these three old friends . . . Remarkably, that chemistry can be heard on *The Odessa Tapes* from the trio's original run."

The *Austin Chronicle* opined, "*Odessa*'s luminous version of Gilmore's 'Dallas' might even be definitive. . . . *The Odessa Tapes* has it all."

A few months after the album's release, *A Prairie Home Companion* tapped them for an episode of the vastly popular show that originated from Lubbock.

David Brown pronounced the album "more vital and more revealing" than the Nashville sessions, calling the music "country, but subversive . . . It placed the band precariously along the cutting edge of some invisible precipice that separated the spirit of old-time music from the soul of rock 'n' roll."

The guys embarked on an extensive tour, both to promote *The Odessa Tapes* and to celebrate forty years of the Flatlanders.

"They took their songs very seriously, but I'm not sure they ever took being a band that seriously," said Lloyd Maines, looking back. "They just enjoyed playing music together."

"This is kind of a full-circle thing," Butch Hancock mused to a Nashville newspaper. He was talking about *The Odessa Tapes*, but he could have been speaking of the wheels-within-wheels perambulations of fate, coincidence, and circumstance that have always characterized the Flatlanders and their journey.

"The album was just us sitting around in a room and playing the music we love the way we love to play it. Just relaxed and doing the bare bones, just the essential stuff to get it across. It's full of Texas, full of the wind. Full of all the love of life and wonder about it all that we could muster at the time, and that's still driving us today."

The *Odessa Tapes* album is the perfect distillation of the Flatlanders' elusive, elemental appeal, a gossamer fabric of words and melody that has its roots in the hard, no-nonsense West Texas earth. It's as transitory as a sunset or a dust storm, as permanent as the Llano Estacado and the vast, blue bowl of sky, and as enduring as a lifelong friendship that is the wellspring for timeless music.

Carnegie Hall

PRACTICE, PRACTICE, PRACTICE

We'd gone through the whole summer, played Kerrville, and the record never came out. . . . They sent a few singles out [but] nobody played it, it was virtually dead in the water. . . .

Fall came around and me and Eddie Beethoven were sitting in the IHOP on 19th Street and decided to go to the Northeast and watch the leaves change color. We were dumbasses. The leaves fell off the trees and we were freezing to death.

We got sucked into New York City. And I was playing downtown, around Wall Street, because we were sleeping on the Staten Island Ferry.

Somebody said you need to go uptown and play around Carnegie Hall, the money will be a lot better there. So we made enough money for a subway ticket, went up and sat out in front, right in the shadow of Carnegie Hall, playing on the sidewalk. So I really did, when I left the Flatlanders in

Lubbock, I went to Carnegie Hall. . . . Now we're back together, and we're going inside the doors, instead of standing outside.

JOE ELY

—————

. . . And on April 13, 2013, they did.

At the zenith of their *Odessa Tapes*/40th Anniversary tour, the guys performed at Zankel Hall in Carnegie Hall as part of the "Late Nights at Zankel Hall" concert series. True, Zankel Hall was a smaller room within the venue, but still . . . Carnegie Hall!

Friends and fans from all over the country flew in to be part of the sold-out show. To the guys it might have just been another day at the office, but to the rapturous audience, it was part graduation, part house party, part surreal wish fulfillment, and part validation.

Lance Webb: I'm their business manager, and I booked the show. The greatest takeaway for me was that the fans felt the guys had achieved something by being able to play Carnegie Hall. It meant something different to each member of the band.

Adrienne Evans-Stark: No one had called Butch initially when they were booked. I think it showed up on Joe's Facebook page, or something. I went and told Butch, "You didn't tell me you're playing Carnegie Hall!" And he went, "I am?" I was jumping around and he was just sitting there jotting notes in his book. I said, "Aren't you excited?" And he was like, "Yeah, it's good."

Joe Ely: There's something inherently humorous about the idea of the Flatlanders playing Carnegie Hall.

Janet Gilmore: I traveled with Adrienne up to New York and when people asked us, we told them our husbands were playing Carnegie Hall. And they would ask, oh, do they play the violin or the piano? Well no, not exactly.

Butch Hancock: My first reaction was, heck, it was just another gig. Which was true. But every time you happen to mention it, everybody goes "Whoa!" Its reputation precedes ours (laughs).

Janet Gilmore: I felt like Cinderella. Friends came from all over the place . . . Ohio, Michigan, Virginia, Austin, Lubbock. In some respects, it was like your own wedding. You wanted to spend time with friends, but you had to tend to business.

Jimmie Gilmore: In one respect, it's a gig, it's a show, and it's not that different from all the other ones in a certain way of looking at it . . . but at the same time, I was deeply appreciative. I never had a goal in my mind that someday I must play Carnegie Hall. But the very words conjure up a feeling for everybody in our culture. And, in fact, the sound was spectacularly good.

Janet Gilmore: For Jimmie, it was a celebration of the music and the friendship.

Lance Webb: As much as Joe's never been concerned with mainstream acceptance of his work, he started on the sidewalk outside and wound up onstage. I think it represented an accomplishment to him.

Joe Ely: Carnegie Hall was the cherry on the sundae. That's a good way to put it.

Butch Hancock: Every gig you play, really, is the best gig in the world, no matter how miserable it is. If you're playing your songs and four people show up—this is fantastic. Or, hey, I'm in Carnegie Hall—*this* is fantastic!

Robbie Gjersoe (Flatlanders' guitarist): Those guys have a way of being not too nostalgic, so the jokes were flying. Like the old one about how do you get to Carnegie Hall? Their joke was, "I dunno, I never practiced!" For the next hour, they're riffing on it.

Joe Ely: The real twist is, the night before, we played in Vermont, way up in the mountains, and an ice storm hit. Then the driver was backing up the bus and noticed the brakes didn't work. So there we were, the night before Carnegie Hall, three hundred miles from New York in a little town with no rental cars. We were actually wondering if we were gonna make the show. But the bus driver fortunately had a piece of air hose for the brakes . . . and then the weather kind of backed up and the ice started melting just enough to let us get down the mountain. And sure enough, we made it just in time for sound check the next morning.

Janet Gilmore: The guys got in about nine in the morning. Adrienne and I and some friends went to the 9/11 memorial. We went out, just the Flatlanders, and had lunch. We all wanted to spend the day together and loosen up. We wanted to take the time to acknowledge and celebrate something that was important to all of us.

Butch Hancock: Nothing about the show really stood out [from a typical Flatlanders show]. We kind of settled on the set, and we did the solo [acoustic trio] set in the middle. That was a little more intimate. Then we broke out of the acoustic set with "Dallas," and that kind of revved things up. . . . Did "Pay the Alligator"—funny to be singing that one anywhere, let alone Carnegie Hall!

Lance Webb: I've seen more than four hundred Flatlanders shows and I've never seen one more perfect than that.

Joe Ely: From the first note we hit onstage, everything was smooth sailing. There had been some confusion backstage, but we hit that first note [of "I Had My Hopes Up High"] and I don't remember much after that. "Hopes Up High" completes a big circle, because I had written that song going to New York, leaving home and catching all those different rides.

Adrienne Evans-Stark: I think the first song was "I Had My Hopes Up High." Butch played "Thank God for the Road," a very spiritual song to me. "Bluebird," "Homeland Refugee" . . . Joe's "Not That Much Has Changed." Butch played "Dangling Diamond," a song from his new album. They only could play one encore, "Midnight Train," because of the curfew and union rules.

Butch Hancock: We're up there enjoying the songs ourselves!

Robbie Gjersoe: The tendency is to say "Carnegie-Schmarnegie," but at the same time, it's New York, it's Carnegie Hall. The sound was phenomenal; it was a joy. Their songs resonated as well as Stravinsky in that hall. There was a sense of, wow, this is really cool, but it's not going to overwhelm us. We'll do our show.

Sharon Ely: My favorite part was Joe saying he had his lovely daughter and wife out in the audience. That was really sweet.

Janet Gilmore: What really surprised [Jimmie and me] was how everybody was celebrating their part in the story. They were there to support the band, but also, something had been validated for them in a way.

Jimmie Dale Gilmore: I really like that idea.

Lance Webb: At Carnegie Hall, what was different for me was you could feel that the audience was so elated that they got to be part of something that was for the band. Like a coronation, of sorts. It was palpable. They were thrilled that the band had made it there. It was like a validation: See, we told you for all these years that these guys deserved this.

Janet Gilmore: You're in this formal environment, so you couldn't jump up and down and scream and holler. People tried to dance and they made them sit down.

Butch Hancock: Some gal stood up and tried to dance in the row of seats, and the ushers had to come and calm her down. No, we can't have dancing in Carnegie Hall. Something ain't right about that!

Jimmie Dale Gilmore: It all felt good. It was one of those ones that went by so fast that I couldn't believe it was over. Three-quarters of the way through the set, and we felt like we'd just started. That's how you know it was a really good show, from our point of view.

Sharon Ely: Not everybody had been there since the beginning, but I had. So to see them play Carnegie Hall and to have heard them for the first time in a living room in Lubbock those many summer nights so long ago . . . it was very spiritual.

Jimmie Dale Gilmore: There was a party afterwards, across the street. Lance might have arranged it or it might have been Janet's idea. Anyway, there was a bar that was serving bar food late.

Sharon Ely: Lance had told them to expect 20 or 30 people and there were, like, 150. Everybody was buying drinks and the credit cards were flyin'! The waitresses were going crazy. But we had a great time.

Robbie Gjersoe: It was a very cool thing that there was so much family there. Leaving the next morning, on the street, there were a lot of wives and kids waving good-bye as the bus pulled out. Family is more than just blood. It's friends and artists and it's all over the world.

Jimmie Dale Gilmore: A few nights later, we were playing in a biker bar in Tennessee. Joe pointed out onstage that last week we were playing in Carnegie Hall and tonight we're here. That was the funniest thing. It kind of shows the way the Flatlanders are.

Butch Hancock: One morning on the way home, we woke up in Texarkana, in this parking lot beside this big drainage ditch on the edge of the ugliest mall I've ever seen. When we stepped out of the bus to get breakfast, me and Joe were kind of rubbing our eyes. We looked at each other and I said, "Joe, weren't we in Carnegie Hall a few days ago?"

Discography

More a Legend Than a Band
ROUNDER, 1990

Arguably, the Rosetta Stone of Americana music. The group's original Nashville recordings, they were a revelation when they surfaced. But the tracks, remixed and overdubbed after the fact, sound a trifle brittle and forced next to *The Odessa Tapes*.

Now Again
NEW WEST, 2002

The group's "sophomore" album—thirty years after the first one—showcases the group's collaborative writing efforts for the first time. The process was eye-opening to them as well.

Wheels of Fortune
NEW WEST, 2004

Ely, Gilmore, and Hancock dip into their respective back catalogs and sample each other's songs, a turnaround from the
all-for-one ethos of *Now Again*. This one rocks harder than its
predecessor, but still retains moments of mellow beauty.

Live '72
NEW WEST, 2004

An artifact from the Flatlanders' summer rambling, between
the Nashville sessions and their eventual parting of the ways.
The sound is all over the map, but the set is noteworthy for
showcasing all the diverse source material the Flatlanders
brought to the table, everyone from Hank Williams to Harry
("Jole Blonde") Choates to Sam Cooke.

Hills and Valleys
NEW WEST, 2009

Hurricane Katrina, the Great Recession, and other real-world
travails thrust themselves into the Flatlanders' musical universe. Once again, the guys collaborate on the lion's share of
the material. "Homeland Refugee" is the greatest song Woody
Guthrie never wrote.

The Odessa Tapes
NEW WEST, 2012

The circle closes. The Flatlanders' original demo tape resur-
faces after forty years. It is a paradox: a warm, breathing,
intimate antique that sounds at once of the moment, and
timeless. This is what friends and lovers heard in that 14th
Street living room so long ago.